HEAVEN
THE PSYCHOLOGY OF THE EMOTIONS
AND HELL

The mind is its own place, and in itself
Can make a Heav'n of Hell, a Hell of Heav'n.

—John Milton, *Paradise Lost*

HEAVEN
THE PSYCHOLOGY OF THE EMOTIONS
AND HELL

NEEL BURTON

Acheron Press

Flectere si nequeo superos
Acheronta movebo

© Acheron Press 2015

Published by Acheron Press

A CIP catalogue record for this book is available from the British Library.

ISBN 978 0 9929127 2 7

Typeset by Phoenix Photosetting, Chatham, Kent, United Kingdom
Printed and bound by SRP Limited, Exeter, Devon, United Kingdom

About Neel Burton

Dr Neel Burton is a psychiatrist, philosopher, writer, and wine-lover who lives and teaches in Oxford, England.

He is the recipient of the Society of Author's Richard Asher Prize, the British Medical Association's Young Authors' Award, the Medical Journalists' Association Open Book Award, and a Gourmand Drinks Award.

www.neelburton.com

About Acheron Press

Acheron Press was established in 2008 by Neel Burton for the purpose of producing and publishing challenging, thought-provoking books without the several constraints of a commercial, sales-driven approach.

The name 'Acheron' was inspired by a verse from Virgil's *Aeneid*:

Flectere si nequeo superos, Acheronta movebo

The line is often translated as, 'If I cannot bend Heaven, I shall move Hell', and was chosen by Freud as the epigraph to his *Interpretation of Dreams*.

According to the psychoanalyst Bruno Bettelheim, the line encapsulates Freud's theory that people who have no control over the outside world turn inward to the underworld of their own minds.

Contents

Preface

With the decline of religion and traditional social structures, our emotions, though maladapted to modern times, have come to assume an increasingly dominant role in our lives. It has forever been said that man is ruled by his emotions, but this today is truer than ever. Yet, remarkably, the emotions are utterly neglected by our system of education, leading to millions of mislived lives. The aim of this book is very simply to help redress the balance.

The bulk of the book is elaborated from a recent series of articles and blog posts on the emotions. The seven chapters on anger, depression, fear, altruism, friendship, love, and courage are adapted from some of my other books, namely, *Hide and Seek*, *The Art of Failure*, and *The Meaning of Madness*. The introduction, though of much interest, is relatively long and technical, and the casual reader may prefer to skip straight to Chapter 1 on boredom. The 29 subject chapters are intended to be read sequentially, beginning with boredom and ending in wonder, but because each is fairly self-contained the reader can easily dip in and out and progress in any order or none at all. As I go on to explain in the introduction, emotions are intimately related to traits, moods, desires, perceptions, and beliefs. For this reason, I have adopted a rather loose definition of 'emotion' and included chapters on, for example, ambition, depression, and lust, as well as a chapter on kissing, which is an emotional expression.

Being aimed also and above all at the general reader, the text aims at clarity and concision and does not purport to offer anything like a comprehensive and balanced account of the psychology of the emotions. If some important emotions are missing from the final list of 29, it is usually because I could not find a particularly interesting or insightful angle from which to approach them. Despite the mounting science, it is impossible and indeed detrimental to remain objective about the emotions, and I have found—not, it has to be said, with surprise—that many of what I consider to be the most penetrating insights on the emotions come not from science but from philosophy, theology, and literature. As ever, I make no apology for leaning heavily on Plato and Aristotle, although I also frequently reference the Bible, Dante, and Shakespeare, among many others.

I hope that you enjoy reading this book as much as I enjoyed writing it, and that it helps you as much as it helped me. To control our emotions is to control ourselves, and to control ourselves is to control our destiny.

Neel Burton
Oxford, June 2015

Introduction

What is an emotion? The answer is not entirely clear. 'Emotion' is a relatively recent term and there are languages that do not carry an equivalent. Historically, people spoke not of emotions but of passions. The passions encompass, or encompassed, not only the emotions, but also pleasure, pain, and desire.

'Passion', like 'passivity', derives from the Latin *patere*, 'to suffer'. It has often seemed that the passive passions are not within our control, and today the term has come to refer to a powerful or compelling feeling or desire (especially love or lust), while also retaining the more restricted mediaeval meaning of the suffering of Christ on the Cross and the martyrdom of the saints.

The notion of passivity is retained in 'emotion', which derives from the Latin *emovere*, 'to move out, remove, agitate'. To *suffer* an emotion is to be acted upon, to be disturbed, and to be afflicted. A long line of thinkers have opposed the 'animal' passions to calm and God-like reason, with various authorities from the Stoics to Spinoza going so far as to advocate *apatheia**, that is, the suppression of feeling, emotion, and concern. Unfortunately, this historical privileging of reason has led not so much to the suppression of feeling as to its near complete disregard. Today, the emotions are so neglected that most people are oblivious to the deep currents that move them, hold them back, and lead them astray.

If I say, "I am grateful", I could mean one of three things: that I am currently feeling grateful for something, that I am generally grateful for that thing, or that I am a grateful kind of person. Similarly, if I say, "I am proud", I could mean that I am currently feeling proud about something, that I am generally proud about that thing, or that I am a proud kind of person. Let us call the first instance (currently feeling proud about something) an emotional experience, the second instance (being generally proud about that thing) an emotion or sentiment, and the third instance (being a proud kind of person), a trait.

It is very common to confuse or amalgamate these three instances, especially the first and the second. But whereas an emotional experience is brief and episodic, an emotion—which may or may not result from accreted emotional experiences—can endure for many years, and, in that time, predispose to a variety of emotional experiences, as well as thoughts, beliefs, desires, and actions. For instance, love can give rise not only to amorous feelings, but also to joy, grief, rage, longing, and jealousy, among others.

---

* *Apatheia* should not be confused with 'apathy'. 'Apathy' derives from *apatheia*, but means the absence, rather than the suppression, of feeling, and is anything but a virtue.

Similarly, it is very common to confuse emotions and feelings. An emotional experience, by virtue of being a conscious experience, is necessarily a feeling, as are physical sensations such as hunger or pain (although not all conscious experiences are also feelings, not, for example, believing or seeing, presumably because they lack a somatic or bodily dimension). By contrast, an emotion, being in some sense latent, can only ever be felt, *sensu stricto*, through the emotional experiences that it gives rise to, even though it might also be discovered through its associated thoughts, beliefs, desires, and actions. Despite these conscious and unconscious manifestations, emotions need not themselves be conscious, and some emotions, such as hating one's mother or being in love with one's best friend, might only be uncovered, let alone admitted, after several years in psychotherapy.

If an emotion remains unconscious, this is often through repression or some other form of self-deception. Of course, self-deception can also take place at the level of an emotional experience if it is not acceptable or tolerable, for example, by misattributing the type or intensity of the emotional experience, or misattributing its object or cause. Thus, envy is often construed as indignation, and *Schadenfreude* (the pleasure derived from the misfortune of others) as sympathy. Fear of ghosts or 'the dark' is almost certainly fear of death, since people who have come to terms with death are hardly frightened of such things. Beyond this, it could be argued that even the purest of emotions is inherently self-deceptive in that it lends weight in our experience to one thing, or some things, over others. In that much, emotions are not objective or neutral perceptions, but subjective 'ways of seeing' that reflect our needs and concerns. I discuss self-deception at length in *Hide and Seek*.

Having distinguished emotions, emotional experiences, and feelings, I ought to say something about traits. A trait is a disposition—or the lack of a disposition, such as pitilessness—to have certain emotions and emotional experiences. Traits also encompass certain characteristic thoughts, beliefs, desires, and actions, and can in turn be shaped by either of these elements. Traits are often named for their predominant emotion and classified as either virtue or vice, for example, humility (virtue), gratitude (virtue), and greed (vice). That said, a number of rather old-fashioned virtues do not involve any one predominant emotion but instead *control* of the emotions, for example, courage, valour, prudence, fortitude, and temperance.

Temperamental traits are innate and cannot altogether be altered, but character traits are more open, or less closed, to shaping. 'Character' derives from the Greek *charaktêr*, which refers to the mark impressed upon a coin, and character traits can become so ingrained as to imprint themselves into our physical features. As Coco Chanel quipped, 'Nature gives you the face you have at twenty. Life shapes the face you have at thirty. But at fifty you get the face you deserve.'

Just as traits can be inferred from behaviour, so behaviour can be inferred from traits. However, situational factors also play an important role in determining our behaviour. In explaining the behaviour of other people, our tendency is to overestimate the role of traits over situational factors—a bias which is reversed when it comes to explaining our own behaviour.* For instance, if Charlotte omits to mow the lawn, I indict her with indolence; but if I omit to mow

---

* This is the correspondence bias or fundamental attribution error. The opposite tendency for our own behaviour is the actor-observer bias.

the lawn, I excuse myself on the grounds of tiredness, bad weather, or some such. Moreover, we are quick to ascribe traits but reluctant to revise our ascriptions in light of accrued information. Even a correctly ascribed trait can be trumped by situational factors, and, of course, has also to contend and compete with any number of other traits.

It can also be instructive to distinguish emotions from moods, desires, perceptions, and beliefs. An emotion is 'intentional' in that it is directed at a specific object or class of object, typically a person or thing, an action or event, or a state of affairs. Note that this object, though specified, need not exist, and it is entirely possible to fear ghosts or love unicorns. In contrast, a mood such as anxiety or irritability is more diffuse and not especially directed at any particular object or class of object. That said, the distinction is not clear-cut: moods can condense into emotions, and emotions evaporate into hanging moods. Indeed, a mood could be described as nothing more than a passive and more or less temporary disposition for emotions of a particular shade or quality—and it is by virtue of this passivity that moods, unlike traits, can be upheld to excuse our behaviour: "Sorry I lashed out. I've been feeling a bit on edge lately." As with emotions, moods have no felt quality other than through the emotional experiences to which they predispose; and so, as with emotions, it is quite possible to be unconscious of a mood and to have it pointed out to us.*

Just as the formal object of belief is truth, so the formal object of emotion is evaluation: beliefs aim at truth, emotions at evaluation. Just like beliefs, emotions aim at being justified, that is, at according with reality. In particular, they aim at reflecting the significance or

---

* This analysis of mood does not extend to mood disorders, which I explore in *The Meaning of Madness*.

meaning of their object for the subject. Desires on the other hand aim at altering reality so that it comes to accord with them. Thus, whereas emotions (and beliefs) have a mind-to-world direction of fit, desires have an opposite world-to-mind direction of fit: emotions aim at reflecting reality, desires at altering it.

Emotions do seem to involve desires. If I am angry with John, surely that is because I desire him to treat me with more respect; if I am scared of the snake, surely that is because I desire to continue living. Emotions also seem to give rise to desires, for example, to scowl at John or to kill the snake with my sabre. Notice, however, that desires of the first kind (desires involved in emotions) differ from desires of the second kind (desires arising from emotions) in that they are more abstract or general or latent, and more akin to dispositions than desires proper.

Desires need not arise from emotions, and come in many forms and shades, including wishes, drives, urges, impulses, compulsions, longings, cravings, and yearnings. Properly speaking, a wish is a desire that is unlikely to be satisfied, as in, "I wish they would just shut up!" A drive is a desire that arises from the body, for example, the sex drive. An urge is a drive that has become urgent. An impulse is a sudden, unconsidered desire that is closely associated with a particular action. A compulsion is an impulse that is difficult or impossible to resist, as in obsessive-compulsive disorder. Longing is a strong and sustained desire, especially for something unattainable or hard to attain. Craving is an uncomfortable longing. And yearning is longing accompanied by tenderness or sadness.

Although perceptions and emotions both aim at reflecting reality, perceptions differ from emotions in important respects. Perceptions are closely associated with sensory modalities and their specialized organs, so any comparison with emotions is at best figurative. Moreover, perceptions are of material objects, and are transparent insofar as they involve nothing more than their object and its physical properties. In contrast, emotions are valenced (positive, negative, or mixed) and can be grounded in mental states other than perceptions, enabling them to be about the past (memory), the future (imagination), or no time at all (fantasy).

Beliefs are thoughts that are held to be true. 'To feel' is often used to mean 'to think' or 'to believe', as in, 'I feel that Bill is lying to me.' The problem with mistaking beliefs for emotions is that this can leave our true emotions unrecognized, in this case, my distrust in Bill or my dislike for Bill. A belief is held, not felt: I can believe that something is fearsome and yet not fear it. Moreover, a belief is either right or wrong, whereas an emotion, however unjustified, is much less open to being contested.

Confusion arises because emotions and beliefs are closely connected. Just as beliefs can give rise to emotions, emotions can give rise to beliefs, and also lend them importance and persistence, which is why Aristotle's *Rhetoric** includes a detailed dissection of the emotions. Significantly, it is emotions that catalyse beliefs into actions. That human beings are much better at making decisions than machines has much to do with our emotions, which define the parameters of any particular deliberation and carry to conscious attention only a small selection of all the available facts and alternatives. Brain injured people with a diminished capacity for emotion find it hard to make decisions, as do people with apathy, which is a symptom of

---

* Rhetoric is the art of persuasion.

severe depression and other mental disorders. Apathy leads to indecision, and indecision to inaction, regardless of the number, nature, or strength of one's beliefs.

So it appears that emotions, although closely related to traits, moods, desires, perceptions, and beliefs, do not amount to any of these things. This suggests that emotions form a separate and natural kind. Yet, the emotions are very varied. For instance, they can be non-moral or moral, non-reflexive or reflexive (about the self, such as embarrassment or guilt), and first-order or second-order (about another emotion, such as shame at my fear). They can also be positive, negative, or—as with, for example, anger or nostalgia—both positive and negative. The only emotion that does not appear to carry a consistent valence is surprise, which can be positive, negative, or mixed—although, of course, every individual instance of surprise is either one or another.

An emotion may be positive or negative by virtue of being pleasant or unpleasant, pleasant emotions, it seems, being reactions to those things that have tended to sustain and confirm us in the course of our evolutionary history, and unpleasant emotions to those things that have tended to undermine us. An important implication is that our emotions may not be entirely adapted to modern life. In particular, our emotions tend to a short-term bias, leading to the hyperbolic discounting of long-term pleasure. In the distant past this short-term bias increased our chances of survival, but with much increased life expectancies has turned into a significant liability. Negative emotions, although generally negative, can become pleasant if their object is a mere simulacrum, which is why some people pay good money to watch horror films or ride rollercoasters, to say nothing of sadomasochism (Chapter 12).

Some emotions, such as humility or nostalgia, are clearly more complex and nuanced than others, for which reason they are not generally attributed to infants and animals. The concept of 'basic' or 'primary' emotions dates back at least to the *Book of Rites*, a first-century Chinese encyclopaedia which identifies seven 'feelings of men': joy, anger, sadness, fear, love, disliking, and liking. In the 20th century, Paul Ekman identified six basic emotions (anger, disgust, fear, happiness, sadness, and surprise) and Robert Plutchik eight, which he grouped into four pairs of polar opposites (joy-sadness, anger-fear, trust-distrust, surprise-anticipation).

It is said that basic emotions evolved in response to the ecological challenges faced by our remote ancestors and are so primitive as to be 'hardwired', with each basic emotion corresponding to a distinct and dedicated neurological circuit. Being hardwired, basic emotions (or 'affect programs') are innate and universal, automatic, and fast, and trigger behaviour with a high survival value. Just yesterday, I opened a cutlery drawer on a large lizard, which, of course, I had not been expecting to find. As the critter darted off into the blackness behind the drawer, I unthinkingly jumped back and slammed the drawer shut. Having done this, I suddenly discovered myself to be feeling hot and alert and primed for further action. This basic fear response is so primitive that even the lizard seemed to share in it, and so automatic as to be 'cognitively impenetrable', that is, unconscious and uncontrollable, and more akin to a reaction than a deliberate action.

One hypothesis is that basic emotions can function as building blocks, with more complex emotions being blends of basic ones. For instance, contempt could amount to a blend of anger and disgust. However, many complex emotions cannot be deconstructed into more basic ones, and the theory does not adequately explain why infants and animals do not share in complex emotions. Instead, it could be that complex emotions are an amalgam of basic emotions and cognitions, with certain combinations being sufficiently common or important to be named in language. Thus, frustration could amount to anger combined with the belief that 'nothing can be done'. Again, many complex emotions resist such analysis. Moreover, 'basic' emotions can themselves result from quite complex cognitions, for instance, Tim's panic upon realizing—or even just believing—that he has slept through an important exam.

Although basic emotions have been compared to programs, it does seem that their potential objects are open to cultural conditioning. If poor Tim fears having missed his exam, this is in large part because of the value that his culture and micro-culture attach to academic success. With more complex emotions, it is the emotion itself (rather than its potential object) that is culturally shaped and constructed. *Schadenfreude* is not common to all peoples in all times. Neither is romantic love, which seems to have emerged in tandem with the novel. In *Madame Bovary*, itself a novel, Gustave Flaubert tells us that Emma Bovary only found out about romantic love through 'the refuse of old lending libraries'. These books, he continues,

> *...were all about love and lovers, damsels in distress swooning in lonely lodges, postillions slaughtered all along the road, horses ridden to death on every page, gloomy forests, troubles of the heart, vows, sobs, tears, kisses, rowing-boats in the moonlight, nightingales in the grove, gentlemen brave as lions and gentle as lambs, too virtuous to be true, invariably well-dressed, and weeping like fountains.*

Cultural conditioning also extends to the expressions of emotion, with some expressions being almost as local as dialects. At the same time, the facial expressions of basic emotions are so resistant to cultural conditioning as to be universally shared and recognized. Indeed, some even extend to certain animals. Expressions of emotion are very varied, and include smiling, frowning, laughing, crying, wailing, jumping back, jumping up, covering the brow, covering the face, kissing, caressing, dancing... Even actions that are not primarily to do with emotional expression can become suffused with emotion, for instance, closing the door (softly or with a slam) or pulling out a pen.

Some expressions of emotion still have functional purposes, for instance, baring the teeth and clenching the fists can serve to intimidate or prepare for attack. In addition, all expressions of emotion serve to signal the emotion—and by extension the evaluation to which the emotion corresponds—to others, forming a system of communication that far antedates language in evolution. In signalling an emotion or evaluation, expressions of emotion aim to inspire the same or a corresponding emotion in others—commonly admiration, sympathy, curiosity, amusement, guilt, or shame.

All this of course implies that others can read our expressions. Our ability to interpret expressions of emotion is quick and unreflective, even with emotions that we ourselves have never experienced or only ever to a mild degree. It relies on the assumption that others share in a psychology that is similar to ours, which is why we exercise caution when dealing with people of a different culture, age, or social class. Since the facial expressions of basic emotions are universally shared, such caution need only extend to the more complex emotions—something, of course, which we subconsciously understand without ever having given it any thought.

Let's take crying as an example of an emotional expression. Human beings shed emotional tears (to be distinguished from basal tears which lubricate and protect the eyes, and reflex tears which flush out irritants) in response to grief but also in response to a range of other emotions such as anger, love, and ecstasy. These tears serve to convey our emotion; to emphasize its depth and sincerity; to attract attention and sympathy at a time of fragility or vulnerability; and, not least by blurring our vision and handicapping our aggressive and defensive capabilities, to signal surrender, appeasement, dependency, or attachment. Given all this, it should come as no surprise that, like other expressions of emotion, crying is often faked to manipulate and deceive—although crocodile tears need not imply evil intentions, and in noble people may even serve a noble purpose.

In many cultures, especially for men, tears of emotion, particularly of grief, are considered undignified or infantile, except in certain circumstances such as mourning the loss of a close friend or relative. After adolescence, men cry far less frequently than women. They also cry for shorter periods at a time and sob much less. Many animals shed basal and reflex tears but only human beings shed emotional tears, so all this snivelling must surely make women more human than men! It has been suggested that some animals, in particular chimpanzees and elephants, can also shed emotional tears, but this is hard to either prove or disprove. Crocodiles on the other hand certainly do not shed emotional tears. The expression 'to shed crocodile tears' derives from an ancient belief that crocodiles cry while ingesting their prey.

Emotions may be tremendously varied, but they are all, by virtue of being emotions, associated with a certain felt quality. For instance, fear is associated with a physiological response involving, among others, a rise in heart rate, increased muscle tension, perspiration, and goose bumps, not to mention expressions of fear such as stiffening of the body, cessation of movement, opening of the eyes, and flaring of the nostrils.

The 19th century polymath William James famously argued that, without such bodily modifications, an emotion would be reduced to 'a cold and neutral state of intellectual perception'. According to the James-Lange theory (named for James and Danish physician Carl Lange), an emotion amounts to no more than the subject's experience of the bodily modifications that arise from the apprehension of an object. Thus, in the words of James, 'we feel sorry because we cry, angry because we strike, afraid because we tremble, and [it is] not that we cry, strike, or tremble, because we are sorry, angry, or fearful, as the case may be.'

Unfortunately, this does seem to be putting the cart before the horse. I am not afraid because I tremble; rather, I tremble because I am afraid. My trembling is not the cause, but a part, of my fearfulness. Moreover, even if there could be enough distinct combinations of bodily modifications to represent and account for every nuanced emotion, it is not at all clear that every emotion need involve bodily modifications, or, conversely, that bodily modifications (for example, during exercise or in illness) need give rise to an emotion. People with high-level spinal cord lesions do not have a reduced capacity for emotion nor a restricted range of emotions, and experimental subjects injected with adrenaline (epinephrine) interpret their arousal differently depending on the type of situation in which they find themselves.

Yet, there is a sense in which the James-Lange theory is correct. Going back to the example of crying, emotional tears can serve yet another purpose, which is to tell us that a particular problem or situation is actually important to us. As markers of strong emotion, tears signal moments of existential importance in our lives, from sharing a first kiss to grieving the loss of our partner. Our tears reveal us to ourselves, and, in so doing, make us more like ourselves—which is why it can be unwise to deny them or hold them back in self-deception.

Emotions can and do involve bodily modifications, perceptions, cognitions, desires, and so on, but, as I have demonstrated, do not amount to any of these, either singly or in combination. An emotion is above all a felt attitude or stance towards an object or class of object. This felt attitude is automatic and often unconscious, and is appropriate or justified if it reflects the relation between object and subject, which itself is a function of context and values. For instance, my anger at my friend's minor misdemeanour is only intelligible in light of my memory of his betrayal, my notions of friendship, the importance that I ascribe to our particular friendship, and many other such factors. Just as an emotion reflects the value placed on an object, so a disposition reflects the value placed on a value. Some dispositions are individually determined, but many if not most are either innate or culturally determined.

An emotion can give us privileged access to an evaluative stance, with the name of the emotion being shorthand for that evaluative stance. However, in many cases, it can be difficult to put a name on an emotion or emotional experience, let alone to fully understand it. First, there are far more emotions than have been named in language. Second, emotions are often blended with other emotions or dominated by some other mental state—for instance, fear is often dominated by the desire or impulse to escape, and only fully felt retrospectively. And third, certain emotions are simply too painful or unacceptable to dwell upon, not least because doing so could give rise to even more difficult emotions.

Our emotions not only reflect and reveal our values, but also enable us to refine them. It is possible to have an emotion about an emotion, and to revise the primary emotion according to the secondary emotion or emotions. Moreover, some of our emotions can feel clear or transparent, while others are more hazy or equivocal. For instance, our love for truth or justice is experienced as profound and authentic, whereas our resentment or disdain for a person of higher virtue or accomplishment lacks resonance and leaves us uneasy.

Like beliefs, emotions are passive insofar as they have a mind-to-world direction of fit. But unlike perceptions, they do more than merely represent the world. Our emotions also represent our values, and if our values are distorted, so are our emotions, leading us to feel and act against our best or long-term interests. Indeed, a single stray emotion can lay waste to the best plans of half a lifetime. It is in this sense that emotions are said to be 'irrational', but, of course, poor feeling is no more irrational than poor thinking. Indeed, poor thinking and poor feeling inexorably lead to each other, and it is, in fact, mostly feeling that drives this deathly dance—hence David Hume's aphorism that 'reason is, and ought only to be the slave of the passions'.

Poor feeling hijacks thinking for self-deception: to hide harsh truths, avoid action, evade responsibility, and, as the existentialists might put it, flee from freedom. Thus, poor feeling is a kind of moral failing, indeed, the deepest kind, and virtue principally consists in correcting and refining our emotions and the values that they reflect.

To feel the right thing is to do the right thing, without any particular need for conscious thought or effort. Conversely, repeated right action can lead to right feeling. Aristotle, the inventor of logic, argued that, in most instances, right feeling, or virtue, is not the product of rational deliberation but merely a matter of habit. In the *Nicomachean Ethics*, he confides that,

> *...if arguments were in themselves enough to make men good, they would justly, as Theognis says, have won very great rewards, and such rewards should have been provided; but as things are, while they seem to have power to encourage and stimulate the generous-minded among our youths, and to make a character which is gently born, and a true lover of what is noble, ready to be possessed by virtue, they are not able to encourage the many to nobility and goodness.*

So unless you are a true lover of what is noble, you may as well stop reading.

1

Boredom

We often forgive those who bore us,
but never those whom we bore.

—La Rochefoucauld

The modern concept of boredom dates back to the 19th century. For Erich Fromm and other thinkers, boredom is a response to industrial society, in which people are required to engage in alienated labour, and to the erosion of traditional structures of meaning.

Yet, it seems that boredom of some form is a human universal. On the walls of the ruins of Pompeii, there is Latin graffiti about boredom that dates back to the first century: 'Wall! I wonder that you haven't fallen down in ruin, when you have to support all the boredom of your inscribers.' Moreover, the mediaeval theologian Thomas Aquinas spoke of an affliction of monks called *acedia*, a state of listlessness or torpor that may have been related to melancholy (Chapter 19). Aquinas opposed this 'sorrow of the world' to spiritual joy, and, revealingly, the 'noonday demon' came to be understood as 'the sin that inspires all other sins'.

So what, exactly, is boredom? Boredom is a deeply unpleasant state of unmet arousal: we are aroused rather than despondent, but, for one or more reasons, our arousal cannot be met or directed. These reasons may be internal or external. Internal reasons include a lack of imagination, motivation, or concentration; external reasons include an absence of environmental stimuli or opportunities. Desiring to engage with something stimulating, we find ourselves unable to do so, and are frustrated by the rising awareness of this inability.

Awareness is key, and may explain why animals, if they do at all get bored, generally have much higher thresholds for boredom. According to writer Colin Wilson, whereas most animals dislike boredom, man, owing to his analytic intelligence, is tormented by it. In man as in animals, boredom is often brought about or aggravated by a lack of control, which is why it is particularly common in children and teenagers, who, as well as being dictated to, lack the mind furnishings to avert boredom, and in employees, who are closely watched and regulated.

Let us dissect a common instance of boredom, such as the boredom that is almost bound to arise from being made to wait in an airport departures lounge. This happened to me just recently, when my flight to Ecuador was delayed for some unannounced reason. I was in a state of high arousal because I was anticipating my arrival in a new and stimulating (and warm!) environment. Although there were plenty of shops and newspapers, I had little interest in either shopping or the news, which would only have succeeded in dividing my attention and so multiplying my boredom. To make matters worse, the situation was completely out of my control, unpredictable (the flight could have been delayed further or even cancelled), and inescapable. As I checked and re-checked the monitor, I became all too aware of all these factors and more. Apart from shops and newspapers, I also had access to copious amounts of alcohol in various forms, but dulling my consciousness would have incapacitated me and falling asleep could have led me to miss my flight. So there I was, stuck in a state of high arousal which I could neither engage nor escape.

Had I needed to catch the flight because my livelihood or the love of my life depended on it, I would have felt much less bored than I did (although much more annoyed). In that much, boredom is an inverse function of need or perceived need. Conversely, if I had not *wanted* to catch the flight (perhaps because I would rather have been going elsewhere or staying at home surrounded by my creature comforts), I would have felt all the more bored and perhaps also upset or angry. As a result, I might have developed an aversion to flying, just like the child who does not want to go to school might develop an aversion to learning.

So far so good, but why exactly is boredom so unpleasant? Philosopher Arthur Schopenhauer argued that, if life were intrinsically meaningful or fulfilling, there could be no such thing as boredom—which may explain why the early Christians conceived of *acedia* as a willful refusal to enjoy the goodness of God and the world that God created. Boredom, therefore, is evidence of the meaninglessness of life. More broadly, boredom opens the curtains on some very uncomfortable thoughts and feelings, which are normally blocked out with a flurry of activity or with more reassuring thoughts or feelings. This is the essence of the manic defence, which consists in preventing feelings of helplessness and despair from entering the conscious mind by occupying it with opposite feelings of euphoria, purposeful activity, and omnipotent control.

People who are prone to boredom are also prone to psychological problems such as depression, overeating, substance misuse, and gambling. Indeed, boredom is so dreadful that we expend considerable resources on its prevention or attenuation. The value of the global entertainment and media industry is poised to top $2 trillion in 2016, and entertainers such as singers, actors, and football players command huge fees and are accorded very high social status. The technological advances of recent years have put an eternity of entertainment at our fingertips, but, paradoxically, this has only made matters worse, in part, by removing us even further both from the moment and from reality. Instead of feeling satiated, we are desensitized and in need of ever more stimulation: ever more war, ever more gore, and ever more hardcore.

So dreaded is boredom that many people would be surprised to learn that it can also have upsides. Boredom can be our way of telling ourselves that we are not spending our time as well as we could, that we should rather be doing something else, something more useful and important, or more enjoyable and fulfilling. And so boredom can act as a signal and stimulus for change, leading us on to better ideas, higher ambitions, and richer opportunities. Most of our achievements, of man's achievements, are born out of an intuitive understanding of boredom. The philosopher Bertrand Russell, who spent some time in prison, went so far as to intimate that prison is the ideal setting for a creative person. For Russell,

A generation that cannot endure boredom will be a generation of little men, of men unduly divorced from the slow process of nature, of men in whom every vital impulse slowly withers as though they were cut flowers in a vase.

There are ways and means of reducing our natural propensity to boredom. If boredom is an awareness of unmet arousal, we can minimize boredom by avoiding situations over which we have little control, cutting out distractions, motivating ourselves, putting things into their proper perspective (realizing how lucky we really are), expecting less, and so on. But rather than fighting a never-ending battle against boredom, let me suggest embracing it. If boredom is a window on the fundamental nature of reality and so on the human condition, then fighting it amounts to pulling the curtains. The night may be pitch black, but the darkness allows us to see far into the stars. For just this reason, many Eastern thinkers go so far as to encourage boredom, seeing it as the path to a higher consciousness. So instead of running from boredom, welcome it, entertain it, and make something out of it. In short, be yourself less boring. Boredom is like the frog of fairy tales: embrace it and it turns into your dream.

The writer Susan Sontag has maintained that boredom is but the reverse side of fascination, since both depend on being outside rather than inside a situation, and the one leads to the other. Instead of being outside a situation, we should learn to get inside it. In *The Miracle of Mindfulness*, the Zen Buddhist Thich Nhat Hanh advocates appending the word 'meditation' to whatever activity it is that we find boring, for example, 'waiting in an airport—meditation'.

In the words of Samuel Johnson,

> *There is nothing, Sir, too little for a creature as man. It is by studying little things that we attain the great art of having as little misery, and as much happiness as possible.*

2

Loneliness

Then stirs the feeling infinite, so felt
In solitude, where we are least alone.

—Lord Byron

People often put boredom down to loneliness, but being surrounded by people who are unstimulating or have become so can itself be a source of boredom—and indeed of loneliness. Loneliness might be defined as a complex and unpleasant emotional response to isolation or lack of companionship. It can be either transient or chronic, and typically includes anxiety about a lack of connectedness or communality.

The pain of loneliness is such that, throughout history, solitary confinement has been used as a form of torture and punishment. More than just painful, loneliness is also damaging. Lonely people eat and drink more, and exercise and sleep less. They are at higher risk of developing psychological problems such as alcoholism, depression, and psychosis, and physical problems such as infection, cancer, and cardiovascular disease.

Loneliness has been described as 'social pain'. Just as physical pain has evolved to signal injury and prevent further injury, so loneliness may have evolved to signal social isolation and stimulate us to seek out social bonds. Human beings are profoundly social animals, and depend on their social group not only for sustenance and protection but also for identity and meaning. Historically and still today, to be alone is to be in mortal danger of losing oneself.

The infant is especially dependent upon others, and loneliness may evoke early fears of neglect and abandonment. In later life, loneliness can be precipitated by breakup, divorce, death, or the sudden loss or undermining of any important long-term relationship. Such a split entails not only the loss of a single meaningful person, but also, in many cases, of that person's entire social circle. Loneliness can also result from disruptive life events such as moving schools, changing jobs, immigrating, getting married, or giving birth; from social problems such as racism or bullying; from psychological states such as shyness, agoraphobia, or depression; and from physical problems that restrict mobility or require special care.

Loneliness is a particular problem of industrial societies. One US study found that, between 1985 and 2004, the proportion of people reporting having no one to confide in almost tripled. In 1985, respondents most frequently reported having three close confidants; by 2004, this number had fallen to nought close confidants. These stark findings may be explained by such factors as smaller household sizes, greater migration, higher media consumption, and longer life expectancy. Large conglomerations built on productivity and consumption at the expense of connection and contemplation can feel profoundly alienating. Aside from being intrinsically isolating, long commutes can undermine community cohesion and compromise time and opportunities for socializing. The internet has become the great comforter, and seems to offer it all: news, knowledge, music, entertainment, shopping, relationships, and even sex. But over time, it stokes envy and longing, confuses our needs and priorities, desensitizes us to violence and suffering, and, by creating a false sense of connectedness, entrenches superficial relationships at the cost of living ones.

Man has evolved over several millennia into one of the most social of all animals. Suddenly, he finds himself apart and alone, not on a mountaintop, in a desert, or on a raft at sea, but in a city of men, in reach but out of touch. Despite our dread of loneliness, our society is highly individualistic and materialistic, so much so that people are no longer called people but 'individuals', and no longer defined according to their social role, needs, or aspirations, but according to their economic function or consumer status. A doctor (from the Latin *docere*, 'to teach', 'to make right') is no longer a doctor but a 'healthcare provider', and his or her patients (from the Latin *patere*, 'to suffer') are no longer patients but 'clients', 'consumers', 'service users' or 'end users'. Anyone with any involvement or interest in their relationship—sorry, 'interaction'—is a 'stakeholder', including investors, creditors, commissioners, managers, administrators, suppliers, collaborators, contributors, commentators, and competitors. These types all train in leadership, communication, negotiation, and conflict handling skills, and organize time and activities for team building, group bonding, and networking. Yet they cannot find the opportunity or humanity to listen, think, or feel, or even to exercise elementary common sense. In March 2013, facing the Health Select Committee to defend his record over the death of patients admitted to Stafford Hospital in Staffordshire, England, the then Chief Executive of the National Health Service (NHS) confessed to Members of Parliament that "during that period, across the NHS as a whole, patients were not the centre of the way the system operated". Instead of contracting yet more hungry management consultants, organizations ought to turn, at least once in a while, to a moral philosopher for perspective and direction.

Some people actively choose to isolate themselves from the rest of society, or, at least, not to actively seek out social interactions. Such 'loners' (the very term is pejorative, implying as it does abnormality and deviousness) may revel in their rich inner life or simply dislike or distrust the company of others. Of course, not all loners choose to be lonely, but many do. Timon of Athens, who lived at around the same time as Plato, began life in wealth, lavishing money upon his flattering friends, and, in accordance with his noble conception of friendship (Chapter 23), never expecting anything in return. When he came down to his last drachma, all his friends deserted him, reducing him to the hard toil of labouring the fields. One day, as he tilled the earth, he uncovered a pot of gold, and his old friends all came piling back. But rather than take them in, he cursed them and drove them away with sticks and clods of earth. He publically declared his hatred of mankind and withdrew into the forest, where, much to his chagrin, people sought him out as some kind of holy man.

Did Timon feel lonely in the forest? Probably not, because he did not believe that he lacked for anything. As he no longer valued his friends or their comradeship, he could not have desired or missed them, even though he may have pined for a better class of man and, in that limited sense, felt lonely. Broadly speaking, loneliness is not so much an objective state of affairs as a subjective state of mind, a function of desired and achieved levels of social interaction and also of type or types of interaction. Lovers often feel lonely in the single absence of their beloved, even when completely surrounded by friends and family. Jilted lovers feel much lonelier than those who are merely apart from their beloved, indicating that loneliness is not merely a matter of interaction, but also of the potential for, or possibility of, interaction. Conversely, it is common to feel lonely within a marriage because the relationship is no longer validating and nurturing us but diminishing us and holding us back. As writer Anton Chekov warned, 'If you are afraid of loneliness, do not marry.' More often than not, marriage results not merely or even mostly from a desire for companionship and intercourse, but also and above all from an urge to flee from our lifelong loneliness and escape from our inescapable demons. Ultimately, loneliness is not the experience of lacking but the experience of living. It is part and parcel of the human condition, and, unless a person is resolved, it can only be a matter of time before it resurfaces, often with a vengeance.

On this account, loneliness is the manifestation of the conflict between our desire for meaning and the absence of meaning from the universe, an absence that is all the more glaring in modern societies which have sacrificed traditional and religious accounts of meaning on the thin altar of truth. So much explains why people with a strong sense of purpose and meaning, or simply with a strong narrative, such as Nelson Mandela or St Anthony of the Desert, are, if not immune, then at least largely protected from loneliness, regardless of the circumstances in which they might find themselves. St Anthony sought out loneliness precisely because he understood that it could bring him closer to the real questions and real value of life. He spent 15 years in a tomb and 20 years in an abandoned fort in the desert before his devotees persuaded him to leave the seclusion of the fort to instruct and organize them, whence his epithet,

'Father of All Monks' ('monk' and 'monastery' derive from the Greek *monos*, 'alone'). Anthony emerged from the fort not ill and emaciated, as everyone had been expecting, but healthy and radiant, and lived on to the grand old age of 105, which in the 4th century must in itself have counted as a minor miracle.

St Anthony did not lead a life of loneliness but one of solitude. Loneliness is the pain of being alone, and is damaging. Solitude is the joy of being alone, and is empowering. Our unconscious requires solitude to process and unravel problems, so much so that our body imposes it upon us each night in the form of sleep. During the daytime, certain people can deliver themselves from the oppression of others by entering into a trance state. This practice tends to be more common in traditional societies, although I have on occasion observed it in my patients. By removing us from the distractions, constraints, and opinions imposed upon us by others, solitude frees us to reconnect with ourselves and generate ideas and meaning. For the philosopher Friedrich Nietzsche, men without solitude are mere slaves because they have no alternative but to parrot culture and society. In contrast, anyone who has unmasked society naturally seeks out solitude, which becomes the source and guarantor of a higher set of values and ambitions. In *The Dawn*, Nietzsche wrote,

> *I go into solitude so as not to drink out of everybody's cistern. When I am among the many I live as the many do, and I do not think I really think. After a time it always seems as if they want to banish my self from myself and rob me of my soul.*

Solitude removes us from the mindless humdrum of everyday life into an eternal and universal consciousness which reconnects us with ourselves and our deepest humanity, and also with the natural world, which quickens into our muse and companion. This distancing enables us to dissociate from earthly concerns and petty emotions, and stimulates problem-solving, creativity, and spirituality. By affording us the opportunity to regulate and adjust our perspectives, solitude enables us to create the strength and security for still greater solitude and the meaning that guards against loneliness.

The life of St Anthony can leave the impression that solitude is at odds with attachment, but this need not be the case so long as the one is not pitted against the other. For poet Rainer Maria Rilke, the highest task of lovers is that each stands guard over the solitude of the other. In *Solitude: A Return to the Self*, psychiatrist Anthony Storr convincingly argues that,

> *The happiest lives are probably those in which neither interpersonal relationships nor impersonal interests are idealized as the only way to salvation. The desire and pursuit of the whole must comprehend both aspects of human nature.*

Be this as it may, not everyone is capable of solitude, and for many aloneness will never amount to anything more than bitter loneliness. Younger people often find aloneness difficult, while older people are less unlikely to seek it out. So much suggests that solitude, the joy of being alone, stems from, as well as promotes, a state of maturity and inner richness.

3

Laziness

I don't think necessity is the mother of invention—invention,
in my opinion, arises directly from idleness, possibly also from
laziness. To save oneself trouble.

—Agatha Christie

Both boredom and loneliness can, under some angles, be looked upon as forms of laziness. We are being lazy if we are able to carry out some activity that we ought to carry out, but are disinclined to do so on account of the effort involved. Instead, we remain idle, carry out the activity perfunctorily, or engage in some other less strenuous or boring activity. In short, we are being lazy if our motivation to spare ourselves effort trumps our motivation to do the right or best or expected thing—assuming, of course, that we know, or think that we know, what that is.

Synonyms for laziness include indolence and sloth. Indolence derives from the Latin *indolentia*, 'without pain' or 'without taking trouble'. Sloth has more moral and spiritual overtones than either laziness or indolence. In the Christian tradition, sloth is one of the seven deadly sins (the other six being lust, gluttony, greed, wrath, envy, and pride) because it undermines society and God's plan and invites all manner of sin. The Bible inveighs against slothfulness, notably in the Book of Ecclesiastes: 'By much slothfulness the building decayeth; and through idleness of the hands the house droppeth through. A feast is made for laughter, and wine maketh merry: but money answereth all things.'

Laziness should not be confused with either procrastination or idleness. To procrastinate—from the Latin *cras*, 'tomorrow'—is to postpone one task in favour of another or others which are perceived as being easier or more pleasurable but which are typically less important or urgent. To postpone a task for constructive or strategic purposes does not amount to procrastination. For a postponement to amount to procrastination, it has to represent poor or ineffective planning and result in a higher overall cost to the procrastinator, for example, in the form of stress, guilt, lost productivity, or lost opportunities. It is one thing to delay a tax return until all the numbers are in, but quite another to delay it so that it upsets our holiday plans and lands us with a fine. Both the lazybones and the procrastinator lack motivation, but unlike the lazybones the procrastinator aspires and intends to complete the task under consideration, and, moreover, eventually does complete it, albeit at a higher cost to himself.

To be idle is, not to be doing anything. Idleness is often romanticized, as epitomized by the Italian expression *dolce far niente* ('it is sweet to do nothing'). Many people tell themselves that they work hard from a desire for idleness. But although our natural instinct is for idleness, most of us find prolonged idleness difficult to bear. Queuing for half an hour in a traffic jam can leave us feeling bored, restless, and irritable, and many motorists prefer to make a detour even if the alternative route is likely to take longer than sitting through the traffic. Recent research suggests that people will find the flimsiest excuse to keep busy, and that they feel happier for keeping busy even when their busyness is imposed upon them. In their research paper, Christopher Hsee and his colleagues surmise that many of our purported goals may be little more than justifications for keeping busy.

We could be idle because we have nothing to do—or rather, because we lack the imagination to think of something to do. If we do evidently have something to do, we could be idle because we are lazy, but also because we are unable to do that thing, or because we have already done it and are resting and recuperating. Lastly, we could be idle because we value idleness or its products above whatever it is we have to do, which is not the same thing as being lazy. Lord Melbourne, Queen Victoria's favourite prime minister, extolled the virtues of 'masterful inactivity'. As chairman and CEO of General Electric, Jack Welch spent an hour each day in what he called 'looking out of the window time'. Adepts of such strategic idleness use their 'idle' moments, among others, to gather inspiration, develop and maintain perspective, sidestep nonsense and pettiness, reduce inefficiency and half-living, and conserve health and stamina for truly important tasks and problems. 'To do nothing at all,' said Oscar Wilde, 'is the most difficult thing in the world, the most difficult and the most intellectual.'

Our nomadic ancestors had to conserve energy to compete for scarce resources and to fight or flee enemies and predators. Expending effort on anything other than short-term advantage could jeopardize their very survival. In any case, in the absence of modern conveniences such as antibiotics, banks, roads, and refrigeration, it made little sense to think long term. Today, mere survival has fallen off the agenda, and, with ever increasing life expectancies, it is long-term strategizing that leads to the best outcomes. Yet, our instinct, which has not caught up, is still for conserving energy, making us reluctant to expend effort on abstract projects with distant and uncertain payoffs. Intelligence and perspective can override instinct, and some people are more future-oriented than others, whom, from the heights of their success, they often deride as 'lazy'. Indeed, laziness has become so intimately associated with poverty and failure that a poor person is commonly presumed to be lazy, no matter how little or much he actually works.

In general, people find it painful to expend effort on long-term goals that do not provide any immediate gratification. For them to embark on a project, they need to believe that the return on their labour is likely to exceed their loss of comfort. The problem is that they tend to distrust and discount a return that is distant or uncertain. People are poor calculators. Tonight they may eat and drink indiscriminately, without factoring in the longer-term consequences for their health, endurance, and appearance, or even tomorrow's hangover. The ancient philosopher Epicurus famously argued that pleasure is the highest good for man. However, he cautioned that not everything that is pleasurable should be pursued, and conversely, not everything that is painful should be avoided. Instead, a kind of hedonistic calculus should be applied to determine which things are most likely to result in the greatest pleasure over time, and it is above all this hedonistic calculus that people are unable to handle.

Many 'lazy' people are not intrinsically lazy, but are so because they have not found what they want to do, or because, for one reason or another, they are not doing it. To make matters worse, the job that pays their bills and fills their best hours may have become so abstract and specialized that they can no longer fully grasp its purpose or product, and, by extension, their part in improving other peoples' lives. A builder can look with aching satisfaction upon the houses that he has built, and a doctor can take pride and joy in the restored health and gratitude of his patients, but an assistant deputy financial controller in a large corporation cannot be at all certain of the effect or end-product of his labour. So why should he bother?

Other factors that can lead to 'laziness' are fear and hopelessness. Some people fear success, or do not have enough self-esteem to feel comfortable with success, and laziness is a way of sabotaging themselves. Shakespeare conveyed this idea much more eloquently and succinctly in *Antony and Cleopatra*: 'Fortune knows we scorn her most when most she offers blows.' Conversely, other people fear failure, and laziness is preferable to failure because it is at one remove. "It's not that I failed, it's that I never tried."

Yet other people are 'lazy' because they understand their situation as being so hopeless that they cannot even begin to think through it, let alone do something about it. As these people are unable to address their situation, it could be argued that they are not truly lazy, and, to some extent, the same could be said of all lazy people. In other words, the very concept of laziness presupposes the ability to choose not to be lazy—that is, presupposes the existence of free will.

I could close with a self-help pep talk or my top-10 tips for overcoming laziness, but, in the longer term, the only way to overcome laziness is to understand its nature and particular cause or causes: to think, think, and think, and over the years, slowly arrive at a better way of living.

4

Embarrassment, shame, and guilt

Where guilt is, rage and courage both abound.

—Ben Jonson

'Embarrassment' is often used interchangeably with 'shame'. Although there is some overlap, embarrassment and shame are distinct constructs.

Embarrassment is the feeling of discomfort experienced when some aspect of ourselves is, or threatens to be, witnessed by or otherwise revealed to others *and* we think that this revelation is likely to undermine the image of ourselves that, for whatever reason or reasons, we seek to project to those others. Potential sources of embarrassment vary according to circumstances, and, in particular, to the company in which we find ourselves. They include particular thoughts, feelings, or dispositions; actions or behaviours such as belching or nose picking; conditions or states such as a bodily blemish or an open fly; possessions such as our car or house; and relations such as our oafish partner, criminal uncle, lecherous aunt, or insolent child. Sources of embarrassment need not be beneath our projected image, but merely out of keeping with it—which explains why it is possible to be embarrassed by our posh parents or rarefied education.

Whereas embarrassment is a response to something that threatens our projected image but is otherwise morally neutral, shame is a response to something that is morally wrong or reprehensible. Shame is normally accentuated if its object is exposed, but, unlike embarrassment, also attaches to a thought or action that remains undisclosed and undiscoverable to others. Embarrassment can be intense, but shame is a more substantial feeling in that it pertains to our moral character and not merely to our social character or image.

Shame arises from measuring our actions against moral standards and discovering that they fall short. If our actions fall short and we fail to notice, we can 'be shamed' or made to notice. If, having been made to notice we do not much mind, we can be said to be shameless or to 'have no shame'. In the *Nicomachean Ethics*, Aristotle points out that shame also arises from lacking in honourable things shared by others like us, especially if the lack is our own fault and therefore owes to our moral badness. Finally, it is possible to feel shame vicariously, that is, to share in the shame of another person or feel shame on his behalf, particularly if he is closely allied or associated with us. Thus, even virtuous people with no personal cause for it can experience shame, and so much is also true of embarrassment and other emotions. 'Hell,' said Jean-Paul Sartre, 'is other people.'

'Shame' derives from 'to cover', and is often expressed by a covering gesture over the brow and eyes, a downcast gaze, and a slack posture. Other manifestations of shame include a sense of warmth or heat and mental confusion or paralysis. These signs and symptoms can communicate remorse and contrition, and inspire pity and pardon. Nonetheless, we may prefer to make a secret of our shame, for shame can in itself be shameful—or, to be more precise, embarrassing.

People with low self-esteem are more prone to shame, because, having a poor self-image, they are harsher upon themselves. In some cases, they may defend against shame with blame or contempt, often for the person who incited their shame. Ultimately, this is likely to lead to even deeper shame, and so to even lower self-esteem. While overwhelming shame can be destructive, mild or moderate shame is mostly a force for good, spurring us on to lead more ethical lives.

Whereas shame pertains to a person, guilt pertains to an action or actions, and to blame and remorse. Shame says, "I am bad." Guilt says, "I did something bad." More subtly, shame involves falling short of cultural or societal moral standards, whereas guilt involves falling short of one's own moral standards. Thus, it is entirely possible to feel guilty about actions of which many or most of our peers approve, such as living in luxury, driving an SUV, or eating meat.

Shame and guilt often go hand in hand, which is why they are often confused. For instance, when we injure someone, we often feel bad about having done so (guilt), and, at the same time, feel bad about ourselves (shame). Yet, guilt and shame are distinct emotions. Shame is egodystonic, that is, in conflict with our self-image and the needs and goals of our ego, and high levels of shame are correlated with poor psychological functioning. In particular, eating disorders and many sexual disorders can largely be understood as disorders of shame, as can narcissism, which is sometimes thought of as a defence against shame. Guilt on the other hand is egosyntonic, that is, consistent with our self-image and the needs and goals of our ego, and, unless left to fester, is either unrelated or inversely correlated with poor psychological functioning.

Faced with the same set of circumstances, people with high self-esteem are more prone to guilt than to shame, and more likely to take corrective or redemptive action.

5

Pride

Pride is the constant enemy of love.

—Anna de Noailles

Pride derives from the Latin *prodesse*, 'be useful'. Like embarrassment, shame, and guilt, pride is a reflexive emotion that is strongly influenced by sociocultural norms and values.

Historically, pride has been conceived both as vice and virtue. Pride as vice is close to hubris or vanity. In Ancient Greece, people could be accused of hubris if they placed themselves above the gods or defiled or denigrated them. Many Ancient Greeks believed that hubris led to destruction or *nemesis*. Today, hubris has come to denote an inflated sense of one's status, abilities, or accomplishments, especially when accompanied by haughtiness or arrogance. As it is out of touch with the truth, hubris promotes injustice, conflict, and enmity.

Vanity is similar to hubris, but refers to an inflated sense of self *in the eyes of others*. Vanity derives from the Latin *vanitas*, 'emptiness', 'falseness', or 'foolishness'. In the Book of Ecclesiastes, the phrase *vanitas vanitatum omnia vanitas* is usually rendered as 'vanity of vanities; all is vanity', and refers not to vanity as such but to the transience and futility of earthly goods and pursuits, and, by extension, of human life itself. In the arts, a vanitas—often a painting with prominent symbols of mortality such as a skull, burning candles, or wilting flowers—invites us to broaden our perspectives by reflecting upon the brevity and fragility of our life. Vainglory is an archaic synonym for vanity, but originally meant 'to boast in vain', that is, to boast groundlessly.

Many religions look upon pride, hubris, and vanity as self-idolatry. In the Christian tradition, pride is one of the seven deadly sins. More than that, it is the original and most unforgiveable sin, for it is from pride that the angel Lucifer fell from Heaven (Chapter 7). Pride is the sin most hated by God because it bears all the other sins, blinds us to truth and reason, and removes us from God and His religion. Just as in the Greek tradition, pride leads to *nemesis*: 'Pride goeth before destruction, and an haughty spirit before a fall.' Thus, in art, pride is sometimes symbolized by a figure of death—or else by Narcissus, a peacock, or a naked woman attending to her hair with comb and mirror.

As a virtue, pride is, in the words of Albertanus of Brescia, 'the love of one's own excellence'. More prosaically, pride is the satisfaction, pleasure, exhilaration, or vindication that arises from having our self-image confirmed, either directly through ourselves or indirectly through others—for example, through one of our children or students, or through one of our in-groups (national pride, gay pride, black pride…). The direct or indirect confirmation of someone else's self-image, but not ours, does not lead to pride but to admiration, toleration, indifference, or envy.

If pride is 'the love of one's own excellence', the inverse of pride is shame. 'Shame', which is discussed at greater length in Chapter 4, derives from 'to cover', and is often expressed by a covering gesture over the brow and eyes, a downcast gaze, and a slack posture. Pride in contrast is usually expressed by an expanded or inflated posture with arms raised or rested on the hips, a lifted chin, and a small smile. This proud stance serves as a signal of status, belonging, acceptance, or ownership. It has been observed across different cultures and even in congenitally blind people, indicating that it is innate rather than learnt or imitated. Being in itself a source of pride, pride promotes more of the kind of actions that ignited it, and is associated with self-respect, self-reliance, productivity, creativity, and altruism.

So, on the one hand, pride is the most blinding and unforgivable of sins, and on the other it is a vector of self-realization. I suggest that there are in fact two types of pride: proper pride, which is the virtue, and false or hubristic pride, which is the vice. Proper pride is clearly adaptive, but how can false pride be explained? People who are prone to false pride lack self-esteem, and their hubris is their way of convincing others and themselves that they too are worthy of respect and admiration. Their 'pride' may be a scam or shortcut, but it does do the trick—if at least for now.

Aristotle wrote insightfully on proper pride, or 'greatness of soul' (*megalopsuchia*). In the *Nicomachean Ethics*, he tells us that a person is proud if he both is and thinks himself to be worthy of great things.

Now the man is thought to be proud who thinks himself worthy of great things, being worthy of them; for he who does so beyond his deserts is a fool, but no virtuous man is foolish or silly.

If he is and thinks himself to be worthy of small things he is not proud but temperate.

> *For he who is worthy of little and thinks himself worthy of little is temperate, but not proud; for pride implies greatness, as beauty implies a goodsized body, and little people may be neat and well-proportioned but cannot be beautiful.*

On the other hand, if he thinks himself worthy of more than he is worthy of, he is hubristic or vain; and if he thinks himself worthy of less than he is worthy of, he is pusillanimous. Hubris and pusillanimity are vices, whereas pride and temperance are virtues because (by definition) they reflect the truth about a person's state and potentials. In Aristotelian speak, whereas the proud person is an extreme in respect of the greatness of his claims, he is a mean in respect of their truthfulness and therefore virtuous.

Aristotle, who was writing long before the Christian era, goes on to paint a very flattering—and to Christian and modern sensibilities, provocative—picture of the proud person. A proud person is avid of his just deserts and particularly of honour, 'the prize of virtue and the greatest of external goods'. He is moderately pleased to accept great honours conferred by good people, but utterly despises honours from casual people and on trifling grounds. As a person who deserves more is better, the truly proud person is good, and as he is good, he is also rare. Pride, says Aristotle, is a crown of the virtues: it is not found without them, and it makes them greater.

Aristotle recognizes that the proud person is liable to disdain and despise, but as he thinks rightly, he does so justly, whereas the many disdain and despise at random (or, I would say, to meet their ego

needs). The proud person may be supercilious towards the great
and the good, but he is always unassuming towards ordinary people;
'for it is a difficult and lofty thing to be superior to the former, but
easy to be so to the latter, and a lofty bearing over the former is no
mark of ill-breeding, but among humble people it is as vulgar as a
display of strength against the weak.'

> *Again, it is characteristic of the proud person not to aim at the
> things commonly held in honour, or the things in which others excel;
> to be sluggish and to hold back except where great honour or a great
> work is at stake, and to be [the author] of few deeds, but great and
> notable ones.*

Aristotle then shifts from the descriptive to the prescriptive.

> *He must also be open in his hate and in his love (for to conceal one's
> feelings, i.e. to care less for truth than for what people will think,
> is a coward's part), and must speak and act openly; for he is free
> of speech because he is contemptuous, and he is given to telling the
> truth, except when he speaks in irony to the vulgar.*

6

Humiliation

How many are humiliated who are not humble!

—Bernard of Clairvaux

Embarrassment, shame, guilt, and humiliation all imply the existence of value systems. Whereas shame and guilt are primarily the outcome of self-appraisal, embarrassment and humiliation are primarily the outcome of appraisal by one or several others, even if only in thought or imagination.

One important respect in which humiliation differs from embarrassment is that, whereas we bring embarrassment upon ourselves, humiliation is something that is brought upon us by others. Tommy confides to his teacher that he has not done his homework. He feels embarrassment. The teacher reveals this to the whole class. Now he feels even greater embarrassment. The teacher makes him sit facing into a corner, provoking the laughter of his classmates. This time, he feels humiliation. Had the teacher quietly given Tommy an F grade, he would have felt not humiliated but offended. Offense is primarily cognitive, to do with clashing beliefs and values, whereas humiliation is much more visceral and existential.

Another point of difference between humiliation and embarrassment is that humiliation cuts deeper. Humiliation is traumatic and often hushed up, whereas embarrassment, given enough time, can be sublimed into a humorous anecdote. More fundamentally, humiliation involves abasement of pride and dignity, and with it loss of status and standing. The Latin root of 'humiliation' is 'humus', which translates as 'earth' or 'dirt'. We all make certain status claims, however modest they may be, for instance, 'I am a competent teacher', 'I am a good mother', or 'I am a beloved spouse'. When we are merely embarrassed, our status claims are not undermined—or if they are, they are easily recovered. But when we are humiliated, our status claims cannot so easily be recovered because, in this case, our very authority to make status claims has been called into question. People who are in the process of being humiliated are usually left stunned and speechless, and, more than that, voiceless. When criticizing people, especially people with low self-esteem, we must take care not to attack their authority to make the status claims that they make.

In short, humiliation is the public failure of one's status claims. Their *private* failure amounts not to humiliation but to painful self-realization. Potentially humiliating episodes ought to be kept as private as possible. Being rejected by a secret love interest may be crushing, but it is not humiliating. On the other hand, being casually cheated upon by one's spouse and this becoming public or even general knowledge, as happened to Anne Sinclair with Dominique Strauss-Kahn, is highly humiliating. Note that humiliation need not be accompanied by shame. For instance, Jesus may have been crucified and thereby humiliated, but he surely did not feel any shame. Highly secure or self-confident people who believe that they are in the right rarely feel shame at their humiliation.

Just as Jesus' crucifixion left stigmata, so humiliation is stigmatizing. People who have been humiliated carry the mark of their humiliation, and are thought of and remembered by their humiliation. In a very real sense, they become their humiliation. After all, who is Dominique Strauss-Kahn today? He is remembered much more for his humiliation than for having been a leading French politician or the director of the International Monetary Fund.

To humiliate someone is to assert power over him by denying and destroying his status claims. To this day, humiliation remains a common form of punishment, abuse, and oppression; conversely, the dread of humiliation is a strong deterrent against crime. History has devised many forms of humiliating mob punishments. The last recorded use in England of the pillory dates back to 1830, and of stocks to 1872. Pillories and stocks immobilized victims in an uncomfortable and degrading position while people gathered excitedly to taunt, tease, and abuse them. Tarring and feathering, used in feudal Europe and its colonies in the early modern period, involved covering victims with hot tar and feathers before parading them on a cart or wooden rail.

Ritual humiliation in traditional societies can serve to enforce a particular social order, or, as also with hazing rituals, to emphasize that the group takes precedence over its individual members. Many tribal societies feature complex initiation rites designed to defuse the threat posed by fit and fertile young men to the male gerontocracy. These rites often include painful and bloody circumcision, which is, of course, symbolic of castration.

In hierarchical societies, the elites go to great lengths to protect and uphold their honour and reputation, while the common orders submit to prescribed degrees of debasement. As a society becomes more egalitarian, such institutionalized humiliation is increasingly resented and resisted, which can give rise to violent outbursts and even outright revolution. Because elites live by their honour, and because they embody their people and culture, their humiliation can be especially poignant and emblematic.

In early 260, after suffering defeat at the Battle of Edessa, the Roman Emperor Valerian arranged a meeting with Shapur I the Great, the shahanshah ('king of kings') of the Sassanid Empire. Shapur betrayed the truce and seized Valerian, holding him captive for the rest of his life. According to some accounts, such as that of early Christian author Lactantius, Shapur used Valerian as a human footstool when mounting his horse. When Valerian offered Shapur a huge ransom for his release, he was killed either by being flayed alive or forced to swallow molten gold. His body was then skinned and the skin stuffed with straw and displayed as a trophy.

In January 1077, Henry IV, emperor of the Holy Roman Empire, travelled to Canossa Castle in Reggio Emilia, northern Italy, to obtain the revocation of his excommunication from Pope Gregory VII. Before granting Henry the revocation, Gregory made him wait outside the castle on his knees for three days and three nights. Centuries later, the Chancellor of the German Empire Otto von Bismarck coined the expression, 'to go to Canossa', which means 'to submit willingly to humiliation'.

Humiliation need not involve an act of violence or coercion. A person can readily be humiliated through more passive means such as being ignored or overlooked, taken for granted, or denied a certain right or privilege. He can also be humiliated by being rejected, abandoned, abused, betrayed, or used as a means-to-an-end rather than an end-in-himself. Philosopher Immanuel Kant argued that, by virtue of their free will, human beings are ends-in-themselves, with a moral dimension that invests them with dignity and the right to receive ethical treatment. To humiliate someone, that is, to treat him as anything less than an end-in-himself, is thus to deny him of his very humanity.

Humiliation can befall anyone at any time. Chris Huhne, the British Secretary of State (senior minister) for Energy and Climate Change from 2010 to 2012, had long been touted as a potential leader of the Liberal Democrat Party. However, in February 2012 he was charged with perverting the course of justice over a 2003 speeding case. His ex-wife, bent on extracting revenge for the affair that had ended their marriage, publically claimed that he had coerced her into accepting license penalty points on his behalf. Huhne promptly resigned from Cabinet but steadfastly denied the charge. When the trial began in February 2013, he unexpectedly changed his plea to guilty, resigned as a member of Parliament, and left the Privy Council. By the end of this sorry saga, he had traded a seat in Cabinet for a mattress in a prison cell. Every twist and turn of his downfall had been chronicled in the media, which went so far as to publish highly personal text messages between him and his then 18-year-old son that laid bare their fractious relationship. In a video statement for the 2007 Liberal Democrat Party leadership election campaign, Huhne had stated: 'Relationships, including particularly family relationships, are actually the most important things in making people happy and fulfilled.' His humiliation could hardly have been more complete.

When we are humiliated, we can almost feel our heart shriveling. For many months, sometimes many years, we may be preoccupied or obsessed by our humiliation and its real or imagined agents or perpetrators. We may react with anger, fantasies of revenge, sadism, delinquency, or terrorism, among others. We may also internalize the trauma, leading to fear and anxiety, flashbacks, nightmares, sleeplessness, suspicion and paranoia, social isolation, apathy, depression, and suicidal ideation. Severe humiliation can be seen as a fate worse than death in that it destroys our reputation as well as our life, whereas death merely destroys our life. For this reason, inmates who have suffered severe humiliation are routinely placed on suicide watch.

It is in the nature of humiliation that it undermines the victim's ability to defend himself against his aggressor. In any case, anger, violence, and revenge are ineffective responses to humiliation because they do nothing to reverse or repair the damage that has been done. The victim either has to find the strength and self-esteem to come to terms with his humiliation, or, if that proves too difficult, abandon the life that he has built in the hope of starting afresh.

I notice that, throughout this chapter, I have subconsciously chosen to refer to the subject of humiliation as a 'victim'. This suggests that humiliating someone, even a criminal, is rarely, if ever, a proportionate or justified response.

7

Humility

Humility is not thinking less of yourself,
it's thinking of yourself less.

—CS Lewis

Today more than ever, our society encourages navel-gazing and celebrates entitlement and exuberance. Economic interests lie not in humility but in hubris, while to call someone or something 'humble' most often connotes that he or it is simple, contemptible, or of little worth.

The first step in arriving at a definition of humility as applied to persons and their characters is to distinguish humility from modesty. 'Modesty' derives from the Latin *modus*, 'measure' or 'manner'; 'humility', like 'humiliation', derives from the Latin *humus*, 'earth' or 'dirt'. Modesty means restraint in appearance and behaviour: the reluctance to flaunt oneself, to put oneself on display, or to draw attention to oneself. It often implies a certain artfulness and arti-ficiality, perhaps even inauthenticity or hypocrisy. The fictional character of Uriah Heep in Dickens's *David Copperfield* is notable for his obsequiousness and insincerity, often invoking his own 'umbleness' to deceive others as to the true scale of his ambition. Modesty often poses as humility, but, unlike true humility, is skin-deep and external. At best, modesty is no more than good manners.

In contrast, true humility derives from a proper perspective of our human condition: one among billions on a small planet among billions, like a fungus on a crumb of cheese. Of course, it is nearly impossible for human beings to remain this objective for very long, but truly humble people are nonetheless much more conscious of their insignificance, an insignificance which verges on non-existence. A speck of dust does not think itself superior or inferior to another, nor does it concern itself with what other specks of dust might or might not be thinking. Enthralled by the grandeur of existence, the truly humble person lives not for himself or his image or reputation, but for life itself.

Drunk on his humility, the truly humble person can seem arrogant to the generality of men. In 399BC, at the age of 70, Socrates was indicted for offending the Olympian gods and thereby breaking the law against impiety. He was accused of 'studying things in the sky and below the earth', 'making the worse into the stronger argument', and 'teaching these same things to others'. At his trial, Socrates gave a defiant defence, telling the jurors that they ought to be ashamed of their eagerness to possess as much wealth, reputation, and honours as possible, while not caring for or giving thought to wisdom or truth, or the best possible state of their soul. After being convicted and sentenced to death, he turned to face the jurors and said:

> *You think that I was convicted through deficiency of words—I mean, that if I had thought fit to leave nothing undone, nothing unsaid, I might have gained an acquittal. Not so; the deficiency which led to*

my conviction was not of words—certainly not. But I had not the boldness or impudence or inclination to address you as you would have liked me to address you, weeping and wailing and lamenting, and saying and doing many things which you have been accustomed to hearing from others, and which, as I say, are unworthy of me. But I thought that I ought not to do anything common or mean in the hour of danger: nor do I now repent of the manner of my defence, and I would rather die having spoken after my manner, than speak in your manner and live.

Throughout his long life, Socrates, who looked like a tramp, was a paragon of humility. Decades before his trial and execution, his childhood friend Chaerephon asked the Delphic oracle if any man was wiser than Socrates, and received the reply that no one was wiser. To discover the meaning of this divine utterance, Socrates questioned a number of wise men, and in each case concluded, 'I am likely to be wiser than he to this small extent, that I do not think I know what I do not know.' From then on, he dedicated himself to the service of the gods by seeking out anyone who might be wise and, 'if he is not, showing him that he is not.' His student Plato insisted that, although Socrates devoted himself entirely to discussing philosophy, he seldom claimed any real knowledge for himself.

Did Socrates lack in humility at his trial? Did he, paradoxically, behave arrogantly by bragging about his humility? Perhaps he put on an arrogant act because he actually wanted to die, either because he was ill or infirm, or, more plausibly, because he knew that by dying in this way he and his teachings would live on in the mouths of men. Or maybe genuine humility can seem like arrogance to those who truly are arrogant, in which case the humble person may sometimes need to hide his humility, or certain facets of his humility, under a cloak of modesty—which, of course, Socrates was unwilling to do.

To be humble is to subdue our ego so that things are no longer all about us, whereas to be modest is to protect the ego of others so that they do not feel threatened and attack us in return. Because the humble man is in fact very big, he needs to slap on an extra thick veneer of modesty. Socrates is not the only humble person who occasionally comes across as arrogant, and a propensity for such 'arrogance' can be found in many if not most leading artists and thinkers. Even doubting Descartes had his moments. In *La géometrie*, published in 1637 as an appendix to his magnum opus *Discours de la méthode*, he writes, 'I hope that posterity will judge me kindly, not only as to the things which I have explained, but also to those which I have intentionally omitted so as to leave to others the pleasure of discovery.'

If humble people are disinclined to conceal the truth, it is because they are by nature truth seekers. It is often through philosophy that they attained to humility, and, of course, humility invites philosophy. Moreover, owing to the inspiration, motivation, and direction that come from proper perspective, humble people are often highly productive or prolific. So it stands to reason that a person who is both insightful and prolific is more likely to be humble, while one who is stuck in a rut and unable to learn from his mistakes probably thinks too much of, or about, himself.

Religious and spiritual movements are naturally keen to emphasize humility. In Greek mythology, Aidos, the daimona of shame, reverence, and humility, restrained men and women from wrong. Some of the most vivid Greek myths, such as those of Icarus, Oedipus,

Sisyphus, and Tantalus, can be understood as admonitions against hubris, which is the defiance of the gods from excessive pride, and leads to *nemesis*.

In the Christian canon, pride is the original sin, for it is from pride that the angel Lucifer fell out of Heaven. Thus the Book of Isaiah:

> *How are thou fallen from heaven, O Lucifer, son of the morning!*
> *How art thou cut down to the ground, which didst weaken the*
> *nations! For thou hast said in thine heart, I will ascend into heaven,*
> *I will exalt my throne above the stars of God... I will sit also upon*
> *the mount of the congregation, in the sides of the north: I will ascend*
> *above the heights of the clouds; I will be like the most high. Yet thou*
> *shalt be brought down to hell, to the sides of the pit.*

In contrast, the Book of Numbers speaks of Moses as 'a man exceeding meek above all men that dwelt upon earth'. The Book of Proverbs says that 'God opposes the proud but gives grace to the humble', and, in the New Testament, Matthew teaches that, 'Whoever exalts himself will be humbled, and whoever humbles himself will be exalted'. Theologian and philosopher Augustine of Hippo argued that humility is the foundation of all the other virtues, for in the absence of humility there cannot be any other virtue except in mere appearance. He held that, while it was pride that changed angels into devils, it is humility that makes men as angels. 'Do you wish to rise? Begin by descending,' he preached in one of his estimated 8,000 sermons. 'You plan a tower that will pierce the clouds? Lay first the foundation of humility.'

In the Hindu *Bhagavad Gita* ('Song of God'), the god Krishna appears to the archer Arjuna in the midst of the battlefield of Kurukshetra to allay his scruples about engaging in battle and shedding the blood of his cousins the Kauravas. Krishna explains that, whether or not Arjuna goes into battle, all the men on the battlefield are one day destined to die, as are all men. Their deaths are trivial because the spirit in which they share, their human essence, does not depend on their particular forms or incarnations for its continued existence. 'When one sees eternity in things that pass away and infinity in finite things, then one has pure knowledge. But if one merely sees the diversity of things, with their divisions and limitations, then one has impure knowledge.'

In the Buddhist tradition, humility is both a part and a product of the spiritual practice, and is perfected on the path to enlightenment. In Taoism, humility is one of the Three Treasures, or basic virtues, along with compassion and frugality. As for Islam, the very word 'Islam' means 'submission (to the will of God)'.

Despite its central place in religion, humility is far from universally acclaimed. Aristotle omitted it from his list of virtues, which does however include 'proper pride' (Chapter 5) and 'proper ambition'. Hume and Nietzsche went so far as to condemn it, and not in the slightest of terms. In *An Enquiry Concerning the Principles of Morals*, the normally cool-headed Hume writes:

> *Celibacy, fasting, penance, mortification, self-denial, humility, silence, solitude, and the whole train of monkish virtues; for what reason are they everywhere rejected by men of sense, but because they serve to no manner of purpose; neither advance a man's fortune in the world, nor render him a more valuable member of society; neither qualify him for the entertainment of company, nor increase his power of self-enjoyment? We observe, on the contrary, that they*

cross all these desirable ends; stupify [sic.] the understanding and harden the heart, obscure the fancy and sour the temper. We justly, therefore, transfer them to the opposite column, and place them in the catalogue of vices...

Hume is tame compared to Nietzsche, who maintained that modern society represents the triumph of Judeo-Christian slave morality over Greco-Roman master morality. For Nietzsche, master morality originates in the strong, and is characterized by such values as nobility, pride, courage, truthfulness, and trust. In contrast, slave morality is merely a reaction in the weak to oppression by the strong, and is characterized by such values as humility, sympathy, cowardice, and pettiness. With master morality, the good is whatever is good for the strong; with slave morality, it is whatever opposes the masters. By pretending that congenital weakness is a choice that is moral and desirable, slave morality makes a virtue out of meekness, impotence, and subjugation. Pride is turned into a vice or sin, humility is exalted as virtue, and the son of God washes the feet of his disciples and allows himself to be crucified like a common criminal. Slave morality is a hypocritical, pessimistic, and destructive inverse morality, a subtle and artful subversion of the old master morality. It seeks not to transcend master morality, but, through 'priestly vindictiveness', to emasculate and enslave the strong by persuading them that their strengths are evil. Today, the old and natural Greco-Roman morality vies alongside the inverted Judeo-Christian morality, which, over time, has taken on the garb of social democracy. Modern man is confused because he constantly has to juggle their contradictions while himself being neither ancient nor Christian.

While there is much of interest in Nietzsche's master-slave dichotomy, he and Hume seem to confound humility with modesty or meekness. Both modesty and humility involve self-abnegation, it is true, but whereas the self-abnegation of modesty is for the sake of others or their regard, the self-abnegation of humility is for the sake of truth and of a higher self.

Indeed, emerging empirical evidence suggests that, rather than being inhibiting, humility is a highly adaptive trait or construct. Scientists have linked it to pro-social dispositions such as self-control, gratitude, generosity, tolerance, forgivingness, and cooperativeness; and associated it not only with better social relationships, as might be expected, but also with improved health outcomes, better academic and job performance, and even a more effective leadership style.

By de-emphasizing the self, humility diminishes the need for self-deception, which in turn frees us to admit to and learn from our mistakes, consider and contemplate alternative possibilities, recognize the qualities and contributions of others, and respect and value sources of legitimate authority. Compared to skin-deep modesty, humility is far more stable and resilient, and so unlikely to crumble under pressure when it is most needed.

In sum, humility could not be more different from mere modesty. If it does resemble anything, then that is the ancient concept of piety, or right relations, but stripped of piety's more concrete religious dimensions.

8

Gratitude

I would maintain that thanks are the highest form of thought, and that gratitude is happiness doubled by wonder.

—GK Chesterton

'Gratitude' derives from the Latin *gratia*, which, depending on the context, translates as 'grace', 'graciousness', or 'gratefulness'. Gratitude never came easily to us men, and is a diminishing virtue in modern times. In our consumerist society, we tend to focus on what we lack, or on what other people have that we do not, whereas gratitude is the feeling of appreciation for what we already have. More than that, it is the recognition that the good in our life can come from something that is outside us and outside our control—be it other people, nature, or a higher power—and that owes little or nothing to us. Gratitude is not a technique or a stratagem, but a complex and refined moral disposition. It has poetically been defined as 'the memory of the heart' (Jean Massieu) and 'the moral memory of mankind' (Georg Simmel).

It is easy enough, both for the debtor and the benefactor, to mistake indebtedness for gratitude. Indebtedness is a much more contained and restricted obligation, or perceived obligation, on the part of the debtor to recompense or otherwise compensate the benefactor, not because recompense is a pleasure, but because obligation is a pain. Unlike gratitude, indebtedness can lead the debtor to avoid and even resent the benefactor. As Seneca said, 'in the case of certain men, the more they owe, the more they hate. A trifling debt makes a man your debtor; a large one makes him an enemy.' Gratitude should also be distinguished from appreciation, which is the recognition and enjoyment of the good qualities of a person or thing, but without the dimension of awe, profundity, or humility that is at the heart of gratitude.

Gratitude is magnified if the conferred benefit is unexpected, or if the benefactor is of a higher social status than the debtor. If a benefit comes to be expected, both it and the benefactor tend to be taken for granted by the beneficiary—a common feature of tired relationships. Gratitude is also magnified if, in benefiting us, the benefactor touched our feelings. If our feelings remain more or less unmoved, we respond not with gratitude but with mere appreciation. Thus, the teachers whom we best remember are not those who taught us the most facts, but those who inspired us and opened us up to ourselves.

Gratitude, by paying homage to something outside us, enables us to connect with something that is larger than ourselves, and that is benevolent and reassuring. By turning us outward, it opens our eyes to the miracle that is life, something to marvel at, revel in, and celebrate, rather than forget, ignore, or take for granted as it flies us by. Gratitude promotes consciousness, enthusiasm, joy, empathy, and tranquillity, while protecting from anxiety, sadness, loneliness, regret, and envy, with which it is fundamentally incompatible. All this it does because it opens us up to a bigger and better perspective, shifting our focus from what we lack or strive for to all that we already have, to the bounty that surrounds us, and, above all, to life itself, which is the fount of all opportunity and possibility. This eagle or godlike perspective frees us to live life, no longer for ourselves, but for life itself.

Cicero called gratitude the greatest of the virtues, and, more than that, the mother of all the other virtues. Today, science has begun to catch up with Cicero. Studies have linked gratitude with increased satisfaction, motivation, and energy; better sleep and health; and reduced stress and sadness. Grateful people are much more engaged with their environment, leading to greater personal growth and self-acceptance, and stronger feelings of purpose, meaning, and specialness.

We can be grateful for likely future benefits as well as past and present benefits. Gratitude for future benefits promotes optimism, and optimism faith. Both Western and Eastern religious traditions emphasize gratitude. In many Christian denominations, the most important rite is the Holy Communion or Eucharist—a term which derives from *eucharistia*, Greek for 'thanksgiving'. Martin Luther himself spoke of gratitude as 'the basic Christian attitude'. More than a mere feeling, Christian gratitude is a virtue, or disposition of the soul, that shapes our thoughts, feelings, and actions, and that is developed, refined, and exercised through a remembered relationship with God and His Creation.

In contrast, ingratitude is ugly and hurtful because it ignores the efforts and sacrifices of the benefactor, thereby affronting him and, by extension, life itself. In Shakespeare's *King Lear*, Lear says:

Ingratitude, thou marble-hearted fiend,
More hideous when thou show'st thee in a child
Than the sea monster!
...
How sharper than a serpent's tooth it is
To have a thankless child!

Hume maintains that 'of all the crimes that human creatures are capable of committing, the most horrid and unnatural is ingratitude, especially when it is committed against parents...' For Kant, ingratitude is, quite simply, 'the essence of vileness'.

Ingratitude, which, of course, has become the norm in our society, corrodes social bonds and undermines public trust, leading to societies built on rights and entitlements rather than duties and obligations, on *me* rather than *us*, and in which every aspect of human life has to be regulated, recorded, monitored, and managed.

Despite the great and many benefits that it confers, gratitude is hard to cultivate. It opposes itself to some deeply ingrained human traits, in particular, our striving to better our lot, our need to feel in control of our destiny, our propensity to credit ourselves for our successes while blaming others for our failures, and our unconscious belief in some sort of cosmic equality or justice. Gratitude is vanishing from our lives because, more and more, we seek to exist as independent individuals rather than as a social collective, and gratitude undermines our ego illusion.

As human nature does not leave much place for it, gratitude is an attainment of maturity, or, to be more precise, emotional maturity, which can arrive at any age or, more usually, not at all. Children who are taught to parrot 'thank you' mean it even less than their parents do. Many people express gratitude, or a semblance of gratitude, simply because doing so is useful or the 'done thing'. A display of gratitude is good manners, and good manners aim at aping profundity when profundity is lacking.

In contrast, real gratitude is a rare virtue. There is a fable in Aesop about a slave who pulls a thorn out of the paw of a lion. Some time later, the slave and the lion are captured, and the slave is thrown to the lion. The starved lion rushes bounding and roaring toward the slave, but upon recognizing his friend he fawns upon him and licks his hands like a puppy dog. 'Gratitude', concludes Aesop, 'is the sign of noble souls.'

Like all virtues, gratitude requires constant cultivation, until such a day as we can say,

'Thank you for nothing.'

9

Envy

It is in the character of very few men to honour without envy
a friend who has prospered.

—Aeschylus

In *Envy*, Joseph Epstein quipped that, of the deadly sins, only envy is no fun at all. 'Envy' derives from the Latin *invidia*, which means 'non sight'. In the *Divine Comedy*, Dante has the envious labouring under cloaks of lead, their eyelids sewn shut with leaden wire. This etymology suggests that envy either arises from, or results in, a form of blindness—or maybe both.

For envy to take root, three conditions must be met. First, we must be confronted with a person (or persons) with a superior quality, achievement, or possession. Second, we must desire that quality for ourselves, or wish that the other person lacked it. And third, we must be pained by the associated emotion. In sum, envy is the pain caused by the desire for the advantages of others. In *Old Money*, Nelson W. Aldrich Jr. describes the beginning of the pain of envy as, 'the almost frantic sense of emptiness inside oneself, as if the pump of one's heart were sucking on air.'

Envy is mean and miserly, and arguably the most shameful of the deadly sins. Our envy is hardly ever confessed, not even to ourselves. Although the terms are often used interchangeably, envy is not synonymous with jealousy. If envy is the pain caused by the desire for the advantages of others, jealousy is the pain caused by the fear of losing our advantages to others. Jealousy is not circumscribed to the romantic sphere, but can also extend to such things as one's friends, reputation, beauty, virginity, and so on. Compared to envy, jealousy is a lesser evil, and therefore easier to confess.

Envy is deeply ingrained in the human psyche, and common to all times and peoples. Our tribal ancestors lived in fear of arousing the envy of the gods by their pride or good fortune. In Greek mythology, it is Hera's envy for Aphrodite that sets off the Trojan War. According to the Book of Wisdom, it is 'through the devil's envy that death entered the world'. According to the Book of Genesis, it is from envy that Cain murdered his brother Abel. And according to the Hindu *Mahabharata*, it is from burning envy that Duryodhana waged war against his cousins the Pandavas.

Envy is especially directed at those with whom we compare ourselves, such as our neighbours and relatives. As Bertrand Russell said, 'Beggars do not envy millionaires, though of course they will envy other beggars who are more successful.' Our age of equality and mass media encourages us to compare ourselves to anyone and everyone, fanning the flames of our envy; and by emphasizing the material and tangible over the spiritual and invisible, our culture of empiricism and consumerism has removed the one countervailing force capable of smothering those flames.

The pain of envy is not caused by the desire for the advantages of others *per se*, but by the feeling of inferiority and frustration occasioned by their lack in ourselves. The distraction of envy and the dread of arousing it in others paradoxically holds us back from achieving our fullest potential. Envy also costs us friends and allies, and, more generally, tempers, restrains, and undermines even our closest relationships. In some cases, it can even lead to acts of sabotage, as with the child who breaks the toy that he knows he cannot have. Over time, our anguish and bitterness can lead to physical health problems such as infections, cardiovascular diseases, and cancers; and mental health problems such as depression, anxiety, and insomnia. We are, quite literally, consumed by envy.

Envy can also lead to some rather more subtle defensive reactions such as ingratitude, irony, scorn, snobbery, and narcissism, which all have in common the use of contempt to minimize the existential threat that can be posed by the advantages of others. Another common defense against envy is to incite it in those whom we would envy, reasoning that, if they envy us, we have no reason to envy them. Bottled up envy can morph into *ressentiment*, which is, in essence, projected envy: the reassignment of the pain that accompanies our sense of failure or inferiority onto a scapegoat, which can then be blamed for our ills, persecuted, and, in the end, sacrificed. Examples of such scapegoats include Marie Antoinette, the Austrian queen consort of France, and, much more recently, white farmers in Zimbabwe.

Though carefully disguised, envy is often betrayed through indirect expressions. *Schadenfreude*, which literally means 'harm-joy' in German, can be defined as pleasure at the misfortune of others. *Schadenfreude* helps to sell the news, which is riddled with stories of disgraced politicians and fallen celebrities. Although the term is relatively recent, the emotion that it denotes dates back at least to the Ancient Greeks. In the *Rhetoric*, Aristotle called it *epikhaireka-kia*, which has the demerit of being even harder to pronounce than *Schadenfreude*. But whatever we call it, the Hebrew Book of Proverbs explicitly warns against it:

> *Rejoice not when thine enemy falleth, and let not thine heart be glad when he stumbleth: Lest the Lord see it, and it displease him, and he turn away his wrath from him.*

The fundamental problem with envy is that it blinds us to the bigger picture. As with Cain and Abel, this blindness destroys lives, including our own. When we are in the grips of envy, we are as the captain of a ship who navigates the seas not by the heavenly stars but by the distorted lens of his magnifying glass. The ship turns in every direction, and ends up being taken by rock, reef, or storm. By holding us back, envy makes us even more apt to envy, opening up a vicious spiral of envy. And so, with our eyelids sewn ever more tightly, we lumber through hell under our cloaks of lead.

It has variously been argued that envy, often under the more respectable guise of compassion or brotherly love, is a force for social change that promotes democracy and equality. The politics of envy ends in communism, which aims at creating a society that is free from envy. In practice, however, those who live under the banner of the sickle and hammer become not less but more envious, going so far as to grass on their neighbours for the slightest of perceived advantages. Just as envy drives communism, so greed (Chapter 10) drives capitalism. Greed too can be fuelled by envy, but at least seeks to level up rather than level down and build rather than destroy.

How to keep a lid on envy? We envy because we are blind to the bigger picture. For example, when we envy our neighbour for his shiny convertible car, we mostly ignore all the efforts and sacrifices that have gone into affording it, to say nothing of the many risks and inconveniences of driving such a car. In the words of Charles Bukowski, 'Never envy a man his lady. Behind it all lays a living hell.' In life, we are rich not only by what we have, but also and mostly by what we do not. It is all too easy to forget that the investment banker or hedge fund manager has effectively sold his soul for his 'success', with so little spirit left in him that he no longer has the vital capacity to enjoy the advantages that he has acquired. Such a man is not to be envied but pitied. To keep a lid on envy, we have to keep on reframing, and reframing requires perspective.

What about the man who inherited his wealth without effort or sacrifice? In the Hindu tradition, 'lucky' people are merely enjoying the fruits of their past karmic actions, including the past karmic actions of their parents, who educated and supported them, and of their grandparents, who educated and supported their parents, and so on. Of course, in some instances, as with the lottery winner, luck really is completely undeserved, making our envy all the more virulent. But inherent in the nature of true luck is that it tends to balance out over time, and so there really is no point in everyone taking turns to envy everyone else. Nature compensates for its shortcomings: if we do not have one thing, we surely have some other, even if it is not the sort of thing that is advertised on billboards. But while we envy, we focus on what we lack rather than what we have and could otherwise be enjoying. Thus, dispositions such as humility (Chapter 7) and gratitude (Chapter 8) can protect against envy.

Envy is also a question of attitude. Whenever we come across someone who is better or more successful than we are, we can react with indifference, joy, admiration, envy, or emulation. Envy is the pain that we feel because others have good things, whereas emulation is the pain that we feel because we ourselves do not have them. This is a subtle but critical difference. By reacting with envy, we prevent ourselves from learning from those who know or understand more than we do, and thereby condemn ourselves to stagnation. But by reacting with emulation, we can ask to be taught, and, through learning, improve our lot. Unlike envy, which is sterile at best and self-defeating at worst, emulation enables us to grow and, in growing, to acquire the advantages that would otherwise have incited our envy. Why can some people rise to emulation, while most seem limited to envy? In the *Rhetoric*, Aristotle says that emulation is felt most of all by those who believe themselves to deserve certain good things that they do not yet have, and most keenly by those with an honourable or noble disposition. In other words, whether we react with envy or emulation is a function of our self-esteem (Chapter 26).

10

Greed

In a consumer society there are inevitably two kinds of slaves:
the prisoners of addiction and the prisoners of envy.

—Ivan Illich

G reed is the excessive desire for more than is needed or deserved, not for the greater good but for one's own selfish interest, and often at the detriment of others and society at large. Greed can be for anything, but is commonly for food, money, possessions, power, fame, status, attention or admiration, and sex. Synonyms of greed include avarice, cupidity, and covetousness.

Greed often has its origins in early negative experiences such as parental inconsistency, neglect, or abuse. In later life, low self-esteem and feelings of anxiety and vulnerability lead the person to fixate on a substitute for what was once needed but absent. The pursuit and accumulation of this substitute fills a void, provides comfort and reassurance, and distracts from uncomfortable thoughts and feelings, with life reduced to little more than a choice between fear and greed.

Greed is much more prominent in man than in other animals, no doubt because man has the unique capacity to project himself in time, and, in particular to the time of his death and beyond. Throughout our short life, our awareness of our own mortality conflicts with our instinct for survival and self-preservation, and gives rise to anxiety about our purpose, meaning, and value. This so-called existential anxiety, which is mostly subconscious, manifests itself in the form of compensatory behaviours, and greed is one such behaviour.

All human cultures elaborate narratives of human life and death to quell our existential anxiety and furnish us with the purpose, meaning, and value that we so crave. Whenever our existential anxiety threatens to surface into our consciousness, we turn to the pillars of our culture for comfort and consolation. It so happens that our culture—or lack of it, for our culture is in a state of flux and crisis—places a high value on materialism and therefore on greed. Our culture's emphasis on greed is so marked that we have become immune to satisfaction. Having acquired one thing, we immediately turn our attention to the next thing that suggests itself to us. Today, the object of our desire is no longer satisfaction, but desire itself.

Another account of greed is that it is programmed into our genes because, in the course of evolution, it has tended to promote survival. Without greed, a person runs the risk of becoming satisfied, and, being satisfied, of lacking the motivation to build or achieve, move or change, leaving him vulnerable, not least to the greed of others. Vulgar though it may be, greed is the only consistent human motivator, and tends to produce preferable economic and social outcomes. In contrast to altruism, which is a mature and refined capability, greed is a visceral and democratic impulse, and ideally suited to our dumbed-down consumer culture. Altruism may attract admiration, but it is greed that our society encourages and rewards, and which delivers the goods and riches upon which we have come to depend. Modern political systems designed to check or eliminate greed have invariably ended in the most abject failure. Our society operates on greed, and without greed would descend into poverty and anarchy. In the film *Wall Street*, Gordon Gekko says:

> *Greed, for the lack of a better word, is good. Greed is right, greed works. Greed clarifies, cuts through, and captures the essence of the evolutionary spirit. Greed, in all of its forms; greed for life, for money, for love, knowledge has marked the upward surge of mankind.*

Economist Milton Friedman argued that the problem of social organization is not to eradicate greed, but to set up an arrangement under which it does the least harm. For Friedman, capitalism is just that kind of system.

While greed may well be good for genes and economies, it may not be so good for individual happiness. A person who is consumed by greed becomes utterly fixated on the object of his greed, with life in all its richness and complexity reduced to little more than an endless quest to accumulate as much money, status, etc. as possible. However much he hoards, he is unable to adapt and reformulate his drives and desires.

If the person is embarrassed by his greed, he may take to concealing it behind a carefully crafted persona. For instance, a man who craves power and runs for political office may deceive others (and perhaps also himself) into thinking that what he actually wants is to help others—for example, by speaking out against those who, like himself, crave power for the sake of power. As well as deception, greed commonly leads to envy and spite. It is also associated with negative emotional states such as stress, exhaustion, anxiety, depression, and despair, and with maladaptive behaviours such as gambling, scavenging, hoarding, trickery, and theft. By overcoming reason, compassion, and love, greed loosens family and community ties and undermines the very values on which society and civilization are founded. Greed may fuel the economy, but, as recent history has made all too clear, unbridled greed can also plunge the economy into a deep recession. Meanwhile, our greedy consumer culture continues to damage the environment, leading to rising sea levels, more frequent extreme weather events, deforestation, desertification, ocean acidification, and species extinctions, among others. What greed can do to a man, it seems to be doing also to the planet. In the longer term, this may not be so good for our genes.

The psychologist Abraham Maslow proposed that healthy human beings have a certain number of needs, and that these needs are arranged in a hierarchy, with some needs (such as physiological and safety needs) being more primitive or basic than others (such as social and ego needs). Maslow's so-called 'hierarchy of needs' is often presented as a five-level pyramid, with higher needs coming into focus only once lower, more basic needs have been met. Maslow called the bottom four levels of the pyramid 'deficiency needs' because a person does not feel anything if they are met. Thus, physiological needs such as eating, drinking, and sleeping are deficiency needs, as are safety needs, social needs such as friendship and sexual intimacy, and ego needs such as self-esteem and recognition. On the other hand, he called the fifth level of the pyramid a 'growth need' because it enables a person to 'self-actualize', that is, to reach his fullest or highest potential as a human being. Once a person has met his deficiency needs, the focus of his anxiety shifts to self-actualization, and he begins—even if only at a sub- or semi-conscious level—to con-template the context and meaning of his life and of life in general. The problem with greed is that it fixes us to one of the lower levels of the pyramid, preventing us from rising to the apex of growth and self-actualization. Of course, this is the precise purpose of greed: to defend against existential anxiety, which is the type of anxiety associated with the point of the pyramid.

Because greed removes us from the bigger picture, because it prevents us from communing with ourselves and with God, it is strongly condemned by all major religious traditions. In the Christian tradition, the deadly sin of avarice is understood as a form of idolatry that forsakes the love of God for the love of the self and of material things, that is, forsakes things eternal for things temporal. In the *Divine Comedy*, Dante has the avaricious bound prostrate on a hard rock floor as a punishment for their attachment to earthly goods and their neglect of higher things. For St Paul, this neglect of higher things is the mother of all sin. *Radix omnium malorum avaritia*: 'greed is the root of all evil'. In the Buddhist tradition, craving holds us back from the path to enlightenment. Similarly, in the *Mahabharata*, Lord Krishna calls covetousness a great destroyer and the foundation of sin:

> *It is covetousness that makes men commit sin. From covetousness proceeds wrath; from covetousness flows lust, and it is from covetousness that loss of judgement, deception, pride, arrogance, and malice, as also vindictiveness, loss of prosperity, loss of virtue, anxiety, and infamy spring. Miserliness, cupidity, desire for every kind of improper act, pride of birth, pride of learning, pride of beauty, pride of wealth, pitilessness for all creatures, malevolence towards all... -all these proceed from covetousness.*

A modern, secular version of this tirade is contained in *The Fear*, a sarcastic song written by American songwriter Greg Kurstin and performed by English singer Lily Allen. Here are a few choice lyrics by way of a conclusion:

> *I want to be rich and I want lots of money*
> *I don't care about clever I don't care about funny*
> *…*
> *And I'm a weapon of massive consumption*
> *And it's not my fault it's how I'm programmed to function*
> *…*
> *Forget about guns and forget ammunition*
> *'Cause I'm killing them all on my own little mission*
> *…*
> *I don't know what's right and what's real anymore*
> *And I don't know how I'm meant to feel anymore*
> *And when do you think it will all become clear?*
> *'Cause I'm being taken over by The Fear*

11

Lust

Lust is to the other passions what the nervous fluid is to life;
it supports them all, lends strength to them all: ambition,
cruelty, avarice, revenge, are all founded on lust.

—Marquis de Sade

Lust can be defined as the strong, passionate longing or desire for certain things: not only sex, but also food, drink, money, fame, power, and knowledge, among others. However, owing to the resonance of Matthew 5:27-28, lust has come to be particularly associated with sexual desire.

> *Ye have heard that it was said by them of old time, Thou shalt not commit adultery: But I say unto you, That whosoever looketh on a woman to lust after her hath committed adultery with her already in his heart.*

There are many reasons for which we can desire sex, for example, to be close to someone, to hold on to or manipulate that person, to hurt a third party, to hurt ourselves, to define our identity, to make a child, or to gain some advantage such as money or security. In the case of lust, sex is contemplated primarily for itself, or, to be more precise, for the pleasure and release that it could procure. However, it is possible to seek out sex for itself without this desire being lustful. For the desire to be lustful, it has to be disordered, that is, inappropriately strong or inappropriately directed. If a person feels lust but does not act upon it, he is lustful without being lecherous; but if he acts upon it, especially repeatedly or habitually, he is both lustful and lecherous.

For Dante, lust was the 'excessive love of others', excessive in that it rivalled and surpassed even the love of God. Romanesque art depicted lust, or carnal luxuria, as a siren or naked woman with snakes biting at her nipples. According to the Church Doctors, luxuria had several daughters, among whom blindness, haste, and self-love. The Church distinguishes lust from fornication, which is having sex with one's spouse for enjoyment rather than procreation, or, more sinful still, having sex outside of wedlock. In Corinthians 7:7, Paul recommends that, to avoid fornication, every man should be allowed to have his own wife, and every woman her own husband.

> But I speak this by permission, and not of commandment. For I would that all men were even as I myself. But every man hath his proper gift of God, one after this manner, and another after that. I say therefore to the unmarried and widows, it is good for them if they abide even as I. But if they cannot contain, let them marry: for it is better to marry than to burn.

While Paul permits (but does not command) marriage, King Solomon, the apocryphal author of Ecclesiastes, seems to warn against it, as well as against lust, on the grounds that they detract from the path to God:

I applied mine heart to know, and to search, and to seek out wisdom, and the reason of things, and to know the wickedness of folly, even of foolishness and madness: And I find more bitter than death the woman, whose heart is snares and nets, and her hands as bands: whoso pleaseth God shall escape her; but the sinner shall be taken by her.

Solomon may be warning against lust and marriage, but he is certainly not warning against misogyny. The fear of lust and its evils no doubt shaped Solomon's attitude towards women, and, through Solomon, the Church's attitude and society's attitude.

King David was undone by his lust for Bathsheba (Solomon's mother), and Bill Clinton, while still the most powerful man in the world, was almost impeached by his lust for a young White House intern. Lust is such a strong and subversive force that it can be very difficult to see through it or see it through. There are many people who couldn't organize a two-ticket tombola, but who suddenly become impressively industrious when it comes to acting out their lust. In the *Divine Comedy*, souls who have committed the sin of lust are blown around in a whirlwind that symbolizes their lack of self-control. Since Dante's time, MRI scanners have revealed that the same area of the brain lights up in people experiencing lust as in addicts receiving their cocaine fix.

Lust is so powerful a force that it is often beyond the power of reason to contain. According to mediaeval lore, when Alexander the Great found Phyllis (by some accounts, his wife) riding Aristotle like a horse around the garden, Alexander exclaimed, 'Master, can this be?' Quick on his feet, Aristotle replied, 'If lust can so overcome wisdom, just think what it could do to a young man like you.'

Shakespeare goes so far as to compare lust to a form of madness, as for instance in Sonnet 129:

> *Past reason hunted, and no sooner had,*
> *Past reason hated, as a swallow'd bait*

No wonder, then, that in Greco-Roman mythology Eros/Cupid is a blind child, and the ithyphallic (erect) satyrs are only half-human. But it is not just that lust can sometimes overcome reason. For Schopenhauer, lust ultimately directs all human behaviour. This is certainly borne out by modern advertising, which seems mostly about suggesting that buying a particular product will help us to obtain the objects of our lust. In contrast, no one ever made a fortune by peddling restraint or wisdom. It is sometimes said that everything is about sex, except for sex itself, which is about power. Even the Church, needing to express the ecstatic communion with God, could do no better than to picture it in terms of an orgasm.

Schopenhauer, who was heavily influenced by Eastern traditions, also drew attention to the misery that is likely to pour out of lust. In the *Bhagavad Gita*, Lord Krishna declares that, along with anger and greed, lust is one of the three gates to Naraka or Hell. When Arjuna asks him by what one is impelled to sinful acts 'even willingly, as if engaged by force', he replies, 'It is lust only, Arjuna, which is born of contact with the material mode of passion and later transformed into wrath, and which is the all-devouring sinful enemy of this world … Therefore, O Arjuna, best of the Bharatas, in the very beginning curb this great symbol of sin—by regulating the senses, and slay this destroyer of knowledge and self-realization…' For the Buddha, lust, in the broader sense of coveting or craving, is at the heart of the Four Noble Truths, which run as follows:

1.   Suffering (*dukkha*) is inherent in all life.
2.   The cause of all suffering is lust.
3.   There is a natural way to eliminate all suffering from one's life.
4.   The Noble Eightfold Path is that way.

Lust, said the Buddha, is controlled or eliminated through attaining a higher consciousness. This idea can also be found sporadically in the Western canon. For instance, poet Charles Baudelaire went so far as to suggest that the artist, who is consciousness personified, ought never to have sex:

> *Only the brute is good at coupling, and copulation is the lyricism of the masses. To copulate is to enter into another—and the artist never emerges from himself.*

As well as being harmful to the subject, lust is harmful also to the object. Lust is the only appetite that is for a person rather than an object, but a person qua object rather than qua person, shorn of uniquely human qualities such as dignity and agency. The lustful person is not only unconcerned about the blossoming of the object of his lust (and perhaps also of the 'old' partner to whom he is being unfaithful), but will act against her best interests to feed his appetite, and with his appetite sated, discard her as 'one casts aside a lemon which has been sucked dry'. These acerbic words belong to Kant, who asserted that a person should never be treated as a means to an end but always as an end in herself. It is perhaps in the nature of lust that it seeks to possess or 'have' the other, to incorporate and degrade the other by destroying his dignity and autonomy. In Kingsley Amis's novel *One Fat Englishman*, the protagonist says that, when it comes to sex, his aim is 'to convert a creature who is cool, dry, calm, articulate, independent, purposeful into a creature who is the opposite of these: to demonstrate to an animal which is pretending not to be an animal that it is an animal.' Of course, there are some people who consciously or unconsciously *want* to be hurt, degraded, or sabotaged, or who feel that they deserve no better, and that is the subject of the next chapter.

Because it is so destructive and subversive, lust is, in the words of Shakespeare, 'a waste of shame'. So as to hide that shame, many cultures magic up a male demon who lays upon sleepers to have sex with them. This incubus (and the less prevalent female equivalent, or succubus) is made to carry the blame for embarrassing nocturnal emissions, disturbing claims of adultery and abuse, and even unexplained children.

Another response to the shame of lust, and much more prevalent in our culture, is to misconstrue lust as romantic love. In contrast to lust, love is respectable, even commendable. We look on approvingly at a pair holding hands or hugging, but we look around for the police if they start acting out their lust. Love is the acceptable face of lust, but the love that is lust in disguise is even more perverse and destructive, and, in that sense, even more shameful, than the lust that knows itself. How to tell lust and love apart? While lust is hasty, furtive, and deceitful, love is patient, measured, and constant. While lust is all about taking, love is all about sharing. While lust is all about using, love is all about building. Lust can lead to love, but it is a poor start and a poor basis, akin to choosing your favourite book by the picture on its cover.

Of course, there is nothing wrong with sexual desire *per se*, and none of us would be here without it. Sexual desire is a life force, to be enjoyed and even celebrated. But, as with wine, the problems begin when it turns from servant into master. It is important to be ready to recognize uncontrolled lust for the blind and destructive force that it is. Uncontrolled lust is especially unattractive in the elderly, because, as the saying goes, there is no fool like an old fool.

Lust is hard to extinguish, but is more readily redirected. If John is angry with his boss, he may go home and act out his anger by smashing some plates, or he may instead run for 30 minutes on a treadmill. This second instance of displacement—running on the treadmill—is an example of sublimation, which is the channelling of unproductive or destructive forces into socially condoned and often constructive activities. As Baudelaire put it, 'the more a man cultivates the arts, the less randy he becomes.'

For Plato, lust is not something to be shunned or shunted, but the first step on the ladder of love. In Plato's *Symposium*, Socrates says that a youth should first be taught to love one beautiful body. By loving one beautiful body, he comes to realize that this beautiful body shares beauty with other beautiful bodies, and thus that it is foolish to love just one beautiful body. In loving all beautiful bodies, the youth learns to appreciate that the beauty of the soul is superior to the beauty of the body, and begins to love those who are beautiful in soul regardless of whether they are also beautiful in body. Once the physical has been transcended, he gradually finds that beautiful practices and customs and the various kinds of knowledge also share in a common beauty. Finally, he is able to experience beauty itself, rather than the various apparitions of beauty. In so doing, he exchanges the various apparitions of virtue for virtue itself, gaining immortality and the love of the gods.

In sum, for Plato, so long as one is willing to learn, lust can be its own cure.

12

Sadomasochism

To fall at the feet of an imperious mistress,
obey her mandates, or implore pardon,
were for me the most exquisite enjoyments…

—Jean-Jacques Rousseau

Sadomasochism can be defined as the giving or receiving of pleasure, often sexual, from the infliction or reception of pain or humiliation. It can feature as an enhancement to sexual pleasure, or, in some cases, as a substitute or *sine qua non*. The infliction of pain is used to incite sexual pleasure, while the simulation of violence can serve to form and express attachment. Sadomasochistic activities are often entered into at the behest of, and for the benefit of, the masochist, who is likely to direct activities through subtle emotional cues.

Consensual sadomasochism should not be confused with acts of sexual aggression. Moreover, while sadomasochists do seek out pain and humiliation in erotic situations, they do not do so in other situations and abhor simple violence and abuse as much as the next person. In short, sadomasochists are not generally psychopaths. Psychopathy, or antisocial personality disorder, is a diagnosable mental disorder, but sadomasochism is not diagnosable unless it causes significant distress or impairment to the individual, or harm to others.

Some surveys suggest that sadistic fantasies are just as prevalent in women as in men. However, it seems that men with sadistic propensities tend to develop them at a younger age. While some sado-masochistic people are purely sadistic and others purely masochistic, many are varying degrees of both, and may describe themselves as 'switchable'. Sadomasochistic practices are very diverse. One study identified four separate sexual themes: hypermasculinity, adminis-tration and receiving of pain, physical restriction, and psychological humiliation. Interestingly, the study found that homosexual males tended more to hypermasculinity, while heterosexual males tended more to humiliation.

Sadomasochism is a portmanteau of 'sadism' and 'masochism', terms coined by the 19th century psychiatrist Richard von Krafft-Ebing, who spoke of basic, natural tendencies to sadism in men, and to masochism in women. He coined the term 'sadism' after the 18th century Marquis de Sade, author of *Justine ou les Malheurs de la vertu*, *Juliette ou les Prospérités du vice*, and other books:

> *How delightful are the pleasures of the imagination! In those delec-table moments, the whole world is ours; not a single creature resists us, we devastate the world, we repopulate it with new objects which, in turn, we immolate. The means to every crime is ours, and we employ them all, we multiply the horror a hundredfold.*

The term 'masochism' he coined after the 19th century Leopold von Sacher-Masoch, author of *Venus in Furs*:

Man is the one who desires, woman the one who is desired. This is woman's entire but decisive advantage. Through man's passions, nature has given man into woman's hands, and the woman who does not know how to make him her subject, her slave, her toy, and how to betray him with a smile in the end is not wise.

While the terms 'sadism' and 'masochism' date from the 19th century, the phenomena they describe are much older. In his *Confessions* of 1782, Jean-Jacques Rousseau bravely admits to the masochistic sexual pleasure he derived from his childhood beatings, adding that, 'after having ventured to say so much, I can shrink from nothing.' Renaissance philosopher Giovanni Pico della Mirandola described a man who needed to be flogged to get aroused. And the *Kama Sutra*, which dates back to 2nd century India, makes mention of consensual erotic scratching, biting, and slapping.

In 1639, physician Johann Heinrich Meibom introduced the first theory of masochism. According to Meibom, flogging a man's back warms the semen in his kidneys, which then flows down into his testicles leading to sexual arousal. Other early theories of masochism made mention of the warming of the blood or the use of sexual arousal to alleviate physical pain. In *Psychopathia Sexualis*, a compendium of sexual case histories and sex-crimes first published in 1886, Krafft-Ebing understood sadism and masochism as stemming from different erotic logics. However, in *Three Essays on the Theory of Sexuality*, published in 1905, Freud observed that people with sadistic tendencies often have masochistic tendencies and vice versa, and so combined the terms. Freud understood sadism as a distortion of the aggressive component of the male sexual instinct, and masochism as a form of sadism against the self, and a graver aberration than simple sadism. He remarked that the tendency to inflict and

receive pain during intercourse is 'the most common and important of all perversions', and ascribed it, as much else, to incomplete
or aberrant psychological development in early childhood. He paid
scant attention to sadomasochism in women, partly because sadism
was thought to occur mainly in men, and partly because masochism
was thought to be the normal and natural inclination of women. In
Studies in the Psychology of Sex, published in six volumes between 1897
and 1928, physician Henry Havelock Ellis argued for the absence of
a clear distinction between aspects of sadism and masochism. He
also restricted sadomasochism to the sphere of eroticism, thereby
divorcing it from abuse and cruelty. Philosopher Gilles Deleuze
begged to differ. In *Coldness and Cruelty*, published in 1967, he
brought the argument full circle, contending that sadomasochism is
an artificial term, and that sadism and masochism are in fact distinct
phenomena. He provided fresh accounts of sadism and masochism,
which, unfortunately, I seem unable to fully understand…

Deleuze may not be entirely to blame. Sadomasochism *is* hard to
understand. Here I propose several interpretations. Many of our
most compelling emotions are the product of more than just one
impulse: while some interpretations may hold in certain circumstances and not others, none are mutually exclusive. Most obviously,
the sadist may derive pleasure from feelings of power, authority,
and control, and from the 'suffering' of the masochist. He may also
harbour an unconscious desire to punish the object of sexual attraction (or, by projection, some other object of sexual attraction, or
objects of sexual attraction in general) for having aroused his desire
and thereby subjugated him, for having frustrated his desire, or for
having provoked his jealousy. By objectifying his partner, who is
thereby rendered subhuman, he does not need to handle her emotional baggage, and can deceive himself that the sex is not all that

meaningful: a mere act of lust rather than an intimate and pregnant act of love. The partner becomes a trophy, a mere plaything, and while one can own a toy and knock it about, one cannot fall in love with it or be injured or betrayed by it. Another interpretation is that sadism represents a kind of scapegoating in which uncomfortable feelings such as anger and guilt are displaced and projected onto another person. Scapegoating is a deep-rooted human impulse. According to the Book of Leviticus, God instructed Moses and Aaron to sacrifice two goats every year. The first goat was to be killed and its blood sprinkled upon the Ark of the Covenant. The High Priest was then to lay his hands upon the second goat and confess the sins of the people. Unlike the first goat, this lucky second goat was not to be killed, but to be released into the wilderness together with its burden of sin, which is why it came to be known as a, or the, scapegoat. The altar that stands in the sanctuary of every church is a symbolic remnant of this sacrificial practice, with the ultimate object of sacrifice being, of course, Jesus himself.

For the masochist, taking on a role of submission and helplessness can be an expression of love and surrender. It can bring back infantile feelings of trust and dependency, fostering a kind of primitive intimacy. In addition, the masochist may derive pleasure from earning the approval of the sadist, commanding his complete attention, and, in a sense, controlling him.

For the dyad, sadomasochism can be understood as a means of intensifying normal sexual relations (among others, pain releases endorphins and other hormones), regressing to a more primal or animal state, testing boundaries, or playing. In her recent book, *Aesthetic Sexuality*, Romana Byrne goes so far as to suggest that sadomasochistic practices can be driven by certain aesthetic goals tied to style, pleasure, and identity, and, as such, can be compared to the creation of art.

'I am human,' said Roman playwright Terence, 'and consider nothing human to be alien to me.' Many 'normal' behaviours such as infantilizing, tickling, and kissing contain recognizable elements of sadomasochism, and in that much each and every one of us can be said to harbour sadomasochistic tendencies. In most dyadic relationships, one partner is more attracted or attached (A) than the other (B). B becomes dominant while A becomes submissive, perhaps even infantilized, in a bid to pacify, please, and seduce. B eventually feels stifled and takes distance, but if he ventures too far A goes cold and shuts out or leaves. This leads to a temporary inversion of roles, with B picking up the chase. The cycle repeats itself until one party —usually B, often because a third party has come along—abandons the relationship. Domination and submission are elements of most relationships, but that does not prevent them from being tedious, sterile, and, to echo Freud, immature. Rather than playing at cat and mouse, lovers need to have the confidence and the courage to rise above that game—and not just by getting married. By learning to trust each other, they can begin to see each other as the fully-fledged human beings that they truly are, ends-in-themselves rather than mere means-to-an-end. True love is about respecting, sharing, nurturing, and enabling, but few people have the capacity or maturity for this kind of equalizing relationship.

And, of course, it takes two not to tango.

13

Desire

Desire is sad.

—W. Somerset Maugham

Desire derives from the Latin *desiderare*, 'to long or wish for', which itself derives from *de sidere*, 'from the stars', suggesting that the original sense of the Latin is something like 'to await what fortune will bring'. According to the Hindu *Rig Veda*, which dates back to the second millennium BC, the universe began, not with light as per the biblical account, but with desire, 'the primal seed and germ of Spirit'. Desires arise in us almost by the second, only to be replaced by further desires. Without this continuous stream of desires, human life would grind to a halt, as it does in people who lose the ability to desire. An acute crisis of desire corresponds to boredom or listlessness (Chapter 1), and a chronic crisis to depression or melancholy (Chapter 19).

It is desire that moves us and lends our life shape and meaning—not meaning in the cosmic sense, but meaning in the more restricted narrative sense. At this moment in time, you are reading these words because, for whatever reason or reasons, you have formed a desire to read them, and this desire motivates you to read them. 'Motivation', like 'emotion', derives from the Latin *movere*, 'to move'. Brain injured people who lack the capacity for emotions find it difficult to decide and desire because they lack a basis for choosing between competing options. Hume famously argued that one cannot derive an 'ought' from an 'is', that is, one cannot deduce or derive moral conclusions from naked facts, and, by extension, that all moral conclusions are grounded in emotion. Though this often escapes our notice, many of our beliefs and all of our desires are born out of our feelings, whether our emotions or sensations such as hunger and pain.

We were born from desire, and cannot remember a time when we were without it. So habituated are we to desiring that, on the whole, we are not conscious of our desires, which only register if they are intense or in conflict with other desires. Meditative practices may not in themselves prevent us from desiring, but they might give us a much better insight into the nature of desire, which, in turn, can help us to disengage from unhelpful desires. 'Freedom', said mystic and philosopher Krishnamurti, 'is not the act of decision but the act of perception.' Try for just one moment to stem your stream of desires. You cannot. Such is the paradox of desire: that even the desire to stop desiring is in itself a desire. This brings to mind the joke about the Zen student who goes to a temple and asks how long it will take him to gain enlightenment if he joins the temple. "Ten years," replies the Zen master. "Well, how about if I work really hard and double my effort?" "Twenty years." To get round the paradox of desire, many Eastern spiritual masters speak of the cessation of desire, or 'enlightenment', not as the culmination of an intentional process but as a mere accident. Spiritual practice, they maintain, does not invariably lead to the cessation of desire but merely makes us more 'accident-prone'.

If desire is life, why should we desire to control desire?—For the simple reason that we desire to control life, or, at least, our life. In Hinduism, desire is both the 'primal seed and germ of Spirit' and the 'great symbol of sin' and 'destroyer of knowledge and self-realization'. Similarly, the second of the Four Noble Truths of Buddhism is that the cause of all suffering is 'lust' in the extended sense of 'coveting' or 'craving'. The Old Testament opens with the cautionary tale of Adam and Eve. Had these earliest of our ancestors not desired to eat from the forbidden tree, they would not have been banished, and had us banished, from the Garden of Eden. In Christianity, four of the seven deadly sins (lust, gluttony, greed, and envy) directly involve desire, and the remaining three (sloth, wrath, and pride) involve it indirectly. Christian rituals such as prayer, fasting, and confession all aim, at least in part, at curbing desire, as does humility and self-abasement, segregation, conformity, communal living, and the promise of life after death.

All suffering can be framed in terms of desire. Raw unmet desire is painful, but so are fear and anxiety, which can be understood in terms of desires about the future, and anger and sadness, which can be understood in terms of desires about the past. The so-called mid-life crisis is nothing if not a crisis of desire, precipitated by the mounting realization that our reality does not bear up to our youthful dreams and desires. If desire can be harmful, so can its objects. The accumulation of houses, cars, and other riches robs us of our time and tranquillity, both in their acquiring and in their keeping. Fame is at least as compromising and inconvenient as it is pleasurable, and can quickly turn into infamy. We need not shun fame and riches, but neither should we set out for them or invest ourselves in them. An excess of desire is, of course, called greed (Chapter 10). Being insatiable, greed binds us to itself, preventing us from appreciating or enjoying all that we already do have, including life itself, which is of all things the most wondrous (Chapter 29).

Desire is intimately connected with pleasure and pain. We feel pleasure at the things that, in the course of human evolution, have tended to promote our survival and reproduction, and pain at those things that have tended to compromise our genes. Pleasurable things such as sugar, sex, and social status are wired to be desirable, painful things to be undesirable. Contentedness and complacency did not favour survival and reproduction. As soon as a desire is satisfied, we stop taking pleasure in its object and turn our attention to formulating and meeting other desires. This is just the problem. Our desires evolved 'merely' to promote our survival and reproduction, not to make us happy or satisfied, to ennoble us, or to give our life any meaning beyond their fulfillment. Nor are they adapted to modern life. Today, survival is no longer our most pressing concern, and, with seven billion people thronging our poor planet, reproduction can seem almost irresponsible. Yet here we are, bonded to our ancestral desires like slaves to their master. Our intellect, in which we have developed a quasi-religious faith, evolved to help us pursue the desirable and avoid the undesirable. It did not evolve to oppose our desires, still less to transcend them. Though we like to pretend otherwise, our intellect is subservient to our desires.

One of the most inspired accounts of desire is that of Schopenhauer. In *The World as Will and Representation*, he argues that beneath the world of appearances lies the world of will, a fundamentally blind process of striving for survival and reproduction. The whole world is a manifestation of will, including the human body. The genitals are objectified sexual impulse, the mouth and digestive tract are objectified hunger, and so on. Everything about us, including even our cognitive faculties evolved for no other purpose than to help us meet the dictates and exigencies of will. Although able to perceive, judge, and reason, our intellect is neither designed nor equipped to pierce through the veil of *mâyâ* ('illusion') and apprehend the true nature of reality. Thus, there is nothing in us that is able to oppose the demands of will, which compels us into a life of inevitable frustration, strife, and pain.

> *Awakened to life out of the night of unconsciousness, the will finds itself an individual, in an endless and boundless world, among innumerable individuals, all striving, suffering, erring; and as if through a troubled dream it hurries back to its old unconsciousness. Yet till then its desires are limitless, its claims inexhaustible, and every satisfied desire gives rise to a new one. No possible satisfaction in the world could suffice to still its longings, set a goal to its infinite cravings, and fill the bottomless abyss of its heart. Then let one consider what as a rule are the satisfactions of any kind that a man obtains. For the most part nothing more than the bare maintenance of this existence itself, extorted day by day with unceasing trouble and constant care in the conflict with want, and with death in prospect...*

It is not so much that we form our desires, but that our desires form in us. Thus, our desires can hardly be said to be 'ours'. We merely infer them, if at all, once they are already fully formed. We infer the desires of a friend from his behaviour, and so it is also with our own. If we are shrewd observers, we may come to know more about our friend's desires than he does himself, particularly if he is defending against his more unacceptable desires by repressing or denying them. If an unacceptable desire nonetheless succeeds in surfacing into his conscious mind, still he may distort or disguise it, for example, by elaborating an entire system of false beliefs to reinvent lust as love. Advertisers exploit this process of rationalization by sowing the seeds of desire into our unconscious mind, and then supplying our conscious mind with 'reasons' with which it can justify 'our' desire.

Schopenhauer compares our conscious or intellect to a lame man who can see, riding on the shoulders of a blind giant. He anticipates Freud by equating the blind giant of will to our unconscious drives and fears, of which our conscious intellect is barely cognizant. For Schopenhauer, the most powerful manifestation of will is the impulse for sex. It is, he says, the will-to-life of the yet unbegotten offspring that draws woman and man together in a delusion of lust and love. But with the task accomplished, their shared delusion fades away and they return to their 'original narrowness and neediness'.

Few of our desires surface into our conscious mind. Those that do, we adopt as our own. But before a desire can surface into our conscious mind, it has to contend with a number of competing and conflicting desires which are all also in some sense 'ours'. Often, the desire that prevails is the one that is at the limit of our understanding. This competitive process of desire formation is most apparent in psychotic people who hear one or several voices that speak from a point of view that seems alien to them, but that is, of course, their own. To quote once again from Schopenhauer:

> *We often don't know what we desire or fear. For years we can have a desire without admitting it to ourselves or even letting it come to clear consciousness, because the intellect is not to know anything about it, since the good opinion we have of ourselves would inevitably suffer thereby. But if the wish is fulfilled, we get to know from our joy, not without a feeling of shame, that this is what we desired.*

That our desires are not truly ours is easy enough to demonstrate. When we make a New Year's resolution, we declare to ourselves and to others that, in some small measure, we are going to take control of our desires, thereby implying that our desires are not normally under our control. The same goes for our vows and promises: but even with the most solemn and public of marriage vows, we often fail to prevail. Indeed, it is often over our most trivial desires, such as what clothes to wear or what music to listen to, that we exercise the most control, while whom we lust for or fall in love with is mostly if not entirely beyond our control. Yet, a single rogue desire can lay waste to the best intelligence of half a lifetime.

In many cases, we simply do not know what we want, and settle with what seems easiest or most fitting. But even when we are sure of what we want, we cannot be sure that it will be good or better for us. A young man may dream of studying medicine at Oxford even if realizing his dream would mean getting hit by a bus in three years' time, or never realizing his far greater potential as a novelist. We should never feel bitter when our desires are frustrated because we can never be sure that what we wanted would have been good or best for us—and judging by the poor quality of our lives, we are obviously very bad at wanting.

Many, indeed most, of our desires simply exist to satisfy other, more fundamental, desires. For instance, if I feel thirsty in the middle of the night and desire a glass of water, I also desire to turn the light on, get out bed, find my slippers, and so on. My desire for water is a so-called terminal desire because it relieves me of the discomfort of thirst; in contrast, all the other desires in the chain are instrumental desires in so far as they aim at fulfilling my terminal desire. In general, terminal desires are generated by emotions and sensations, instrumental desires by intellect. Being generated by emotions and sensations, terminal desires are strongly motivated, while instrumental desires are merely motivated through the terminal desire at which they are directed. The best desires are those that are both terminal and instrumental, as when we work for a living and also enjoy the work that we do.

As well as a terminal desire, my desire for water is a hedonic desire in that it aims at pleasure or the avoidance of pain. Terminal desires are generally hedonic, although some, such as when I do the right thing for the sake of doing the right thing, are motivated by sheer will. One could argue that there can be no such thing as a non-hedonic terminal desire: even when I 'do the right thing for the sake of doing the right thing', I experience pleasure in doing so, or avoid such pains as the pain of guilt, and so my desire is merely a hedonic desire in disguise. Nonetheless, some terminal desires, such as hunger or thirst, are clearly more biological than others, and these tend to be most strongly motivated. More abstract terminal desires are driven by our emotions, and may be less motivated if our emotions fail to back them, or back them but only feebly. Unfortunately, the extent to which an abstract terminal desire is supported by our emotions is completely out of our control. Or as Schopenhauer put it, 'Man can do what he wants but he cannot want what he wants.'

It is of course possible for the intellect to rebel against the emotions or even the sensations and reject a highly motivated terminal desire, but the slave is not as strong as the master and risks being whipped back into his den. Rather than confronting his master head-on, the slave stands a better chance of success if he replaces his master's desire with another or reframes it in the master's own terms, typically by arguing that resisting the desire will lead to greater pleasure over time. The slave can also attempt to trick the master, for instance, by means of a cemetery meditation against lust, which involves imagining the dead body of the lusted-after person in various stages of decomposition.

At last, desires can also be divided into natural and unnatural. Natural desires such as those for food or shelter are naturally limited. In contrast, unnatural or vain desires such as those for fame, power, or wealth are potentially unlimited. Epicurus taught that natural desires, though difficult to eliminate, are both easy and highly pleasurable to satisfy, and should be satisfied. In contrast, unnatural desires are neither easy nor highly pleasurable to satisfy, and should be eliminated. By following this prescription for the selective elimination of desires, a person can minimize the pain and anxiety of harbouring unfulfilled desires, and thereby bring himself as near as possible to *ataraxia* or perfect mental tranquillity. 'If thou wilt make a man happy,' said Epicurus, 'add not unto his riches but take away from his desires.'

Unnatural desires, which are unlimited, have their origins not in nature but in society. Fame, power, and wealth can all be understood in terms of the desire for social status. Were we the last person on earth, being famous, powerful, or wealthy would not only be useless but meaningless. We would desire very differently and, leaving aside our loneliness, would stand a much better chance of satisfaction. As well as unnatural desires, society gives rise to destructive desires such as the desire to make others envy us, and the desire to see others fail (or, at least, not succeed as much as us). Other people become the targets and victims of our insecurities, and we in turn become those of theirs. As Schopenhauer said, 'What every one most aims at in ordinary contact with his fellows is to prove them inferior to himself.' By overcoming the desire to satisfy, please, impress, or outdo others, we can at last begin to live for ourselves, free from unnatural and destructive desires.

Diogenes the Cynic, who was a contemporary of Plato in Ancient Athens, taught by living example that wisdom and happiness belong to the person who is independent of society. After being exiled from his native Sinope for having defaced its coinage, he moved to Athens, took up the life of a beggar, and made it his mission to metaphorically deface the coinage of custom and convention, which, he maintained, was the false coin of morality. He disdained the need for conventional shelter or any other such dainties and elected to live in a tub and survive on a diet of onions. He was not impressed with his fellow men, not even with Alexander the Great, who, it is said, came to meet him one morning while he was lying in the sunshine. When Alexander asked him whether there was any favour he might do for him, he replied, "Yes, stand out of my sunlight." To his credit, Alexander declared, "If I were not Alexander, then I should wish to be Diogenes." Once, upon being asked to name the most beautiful of all things, Diogenes replied *parrhesia*, which means 'free speech' or 'full expression'. He used to stroll around Athens in broad daylight brandishing an ignited lamp. Whenever curious people stopped and asked what he was doing, he would reply, "I am just looking for a human being."

Fortunately, there is no need to imitate Diogenes and still less to banish desire, but, paradoxically, it is only by mastering desire that we can live life to its fullest. And it is only by mastering desire that we might at last find peace.

14

Hope

Hope is the dream of a waking man.

—Aristotle

Hope can be defined as the desire for something to happen combined with an anticipation of it happening. It is the anticipation of something desired. With any hope, the desiring can be more or less strong, as can the anticipation. Thus it is possible to desire something very strongly and yet to believe that it is very unlikely to materialize. That said, desirable things that are more likely to materialize tend to be more strongly desired.

To hope for something is to desire that thing, and to believe, rightly or wrongly, that the probability of it happening, though less than 1, is greater than 0. If the probability of it happening is 1 or very close to 1, it is not a hope but an expectation; if it is 0, it is a fantasy; and if it is very close to 0, it is a wish. Even though hope involves an estimation of probabilities, this rational calculation is often imprecise and unconscious. When we hope, we do not know what the odds, or at least our odds, might be, but still choose to 'hope against hope'. This combination of ignorance and defiance is integral to the meaning of hope.

In Plato's *Protagoras*, Socrates says that the statesman Pericles gave his sons excellent instruction in everything that could be learnt from teachers, but when it came to virtue he simply left them to 'wander at their own free will in a sort of hope that they would light upon virtue of their own accord'. This usage of 'hope' suggests that hoped for things are partly or even largely outside of our personal control.

One opposite of hope is fear, which is the desire for something not to happen combined with an anticipation of it happening. Inherent in every hope is a fear, and in every fear a hope. Other opposites of hope are hopelessness and despair (from the Latin *de-* 'without' + *sperare* 'to hope'), which is an agitated form of hopelessness.

It can be instructive to compare hope with optimism and faith. Hope is more particular and specific, and also more engaged, than optimism, which is a general attitude of hopefulness that everything or most things or many things will turn out for the better or best. To admit to hoping for something is to acknowledge that thing's significance to us, and so to make a claim about ourselves. Aquinas opined that faith has to do with things that are not seen, while hope has to do with things that are not at hand. If hope is more engaged than optimism, faith is more engaged still, so much so that it does not admit of doubt. Faith that is slightly less engaged is called trust.

Hope features prominently in myth and religion. In Aesop's Fables, hope is symbolized by the swallow, which is among the first birds to appear at the close of winter. The moral, 'One swallow does not make a summer' belongs to the fable *The Spendthrift and the Swallow*. A young man, a great spendthrift, had nothing left to his name but one good cloak. One day, he spotted a swallow skimming along a pool and twittering gaily. Supposing that summer had arrived, he set off to the market to sell his cloak. But a few days later, winter returned with renewed frost and snow. Finding the unfortunate swallow lying lifeless on the ground, the spendthrift cried out, "Unhappy bird! what have you done? By thus appearing before the springtime you have not only killed yourself, but you have wrought my destruction also."

In Greek myth, Prometheus stole the secret of fire and gave it to mankind. To punish mankind, Zeus ordered Hephaestus to mold the first woman out of earth and water, and asked each of the gods to endow this creature with a seductive gift. Zeus then gave Pandora ('All-gifted') a jar of evils and sent her off to Prometheus' brother Epimetheus. Although Pandora had been warned not to open the jar, her natural curiosity overcame her and she unsealed the lid, disseminating every evil upon the earth and bringing man's golden age to a close. Pandora hastened to replace the lid, but all the contents of the jar had already escaped—all, that is, but hope, which lay forlorn at the bottom of the jar. Aside from the blatant misogyny, the myth of Pandora is difficult to interpret. It could mean that hope has been preserved to temper our torments; or, to the contrary, that it is has been held back to multiply our misery; or again that it was just one among many evils in the jar, the kind of false and foolish hope that leads us astray and renews our anguish. All three interpretations are in the nature of hope, and so perhaps the ambiguity is deliberate. A fourth and more hopeful interpretation is that hope is only to be found once all our evils have left us.

In Christianity, hope is one of the three theological virtues alongside faith and charity (love)—'theological' because it is born out of the grace of God, and also because it has God for its object. Christian hope is much more than a probabilistic anticipation of something desired. It is a 'confident expectation', a trust in God and His gifts that frees the believer from hesitation, fear, greed, and anything else that might keep him from charity ('love'), which, according to 1 Corinthians 13:13, is the greatest of the three theological virtues. 'But now abideth faith, hope, love, these three; and the greatest of these is love.' Thus, Christian hope is more akin to trust or faith than to hope; it is faith in the future tense. Like prayer, it is an expression of the subject's limitations, and of his connection with and dependence on something other and greater than himself. Hope is attractive and desirable because it is an act of piety and humility (Chapter 7).

The inscription on the gate to hell in Dante's *Inferno* suggests that the Christian concept of hell is marked and perhaps even defined by hopelessness, that is, by the severance of the bond between man and the divine.

Through me you enter the city of woe,
through me you go to everlasting pain,
through me you go among the lost people.

Justice moved my exalted Creator:
by the Holiest Power was I made,
and Supreme Wisdom and Primal Love.

Nothing before I was made was made
but things eternal, and I too am eternal.
Abandon all hope, Ye Who Enter Here!

Back up in the land of the living, there is a saying that, 'there is no life without hope'. Hope is an expression of confidence in life, and the foundation for more practical virtues such as patience, determination, and courage. It provides us not only with goals, but also with the motivation to achieve or attain those goals. As Martin Luther wrote, 'Everything that is done in the world is done by hope.'

Hope also makes present hardship—be it loneliness, betrayal, poverty, sickness, or just the daily commute—less difficult to bear. Even in the unlikely absence of hardship, still hope is needed, for we are not content to be content, and a large part of our contentedness is mortgaged to the prospect of change and advancement.

At a deeper level, hope connects our present to our past and future, and writes the overarching story that lends our life shape and meaning. Our hopes are the strands that run through our years, defining and in some sense ennobling our struggles, our successes and setbacks, and our strengths and shortcomings. To hope is profoundly human, for, of all the animals, only man can project himself into the abstract future. Our hopes not only connect our years, but also connect us with something much greater than ourselves, a cosmic force that inhabits us and inhabits all of nature.

Given all of the above, it should come as no surprise that hopelessness is both a cause and a symptom of depression, and also an important predictor of suicide. "What are you hoping for out of life?" is one of my stock questions as a psychiatrist, and if my patient replies "nothing", I am bound to take that very seriously. Hope is protective and hope is healing, and an important aspect of my clinical work is to somehow re-instill it into my patients.

Hope is pleasurable, because the anticipation of something desired is pleasurable. But hope can also be painful in so far as the desired thing is not at hand, and, moreover, may never be at hand. The pain of hope, and the even greater pain of dashed hope, holds us back from hoping too high. At the same time, a strong desire for something can lead us to overestimate the probability of it happening, and, in particular, of it happening to us. Many if not most of our hopes are less than likely to materialize, but some, such as the hope that our remarried ex might one day return or that scientific progress might enable us to live forever, are more in the realm of wish or fantasy than in the realm of hope, and arguably on the same spectrum as the fanciful delusions of mania. Both reasonable hopes and false hopes lift us up, but whereas reasonable hopes move us on, false hopes hold us back, and in the longer term are bound to lead to frustration, disappointment, and resentment, not to mention embarrassment and ridicule. Relinquishing false hopes can set us free, but freedom is not for everyone, and many people have nothing but their false hopes to keep them afloat on the sea of insanity.

Hope generally gets a bad press from philosophers because it is seen as irrational, undependable, and unstable, and so inimical to the values and self-construct of the philosopher, who yet would not philosophize without the hope that philosophizing might lead him to a desirable end or desirable ends. Existentialist philosophers share in this general disdain, arguing that, by hiding the hard truth of the human condition, hope leads us into a life that is disengaged and inauthentic. Yet, the existentialists also have something very interesting to say about hope. In *The Myth of Sisyphus*, Albert Camus compares the human condition to the plight of Sisyphus, a mythological king of Ephyra punished for his chronic deceitfulness by being made to repeat forever the same meaningless task of pushing a boulder up a mountain, only to see it roll back down again. Camus concludes, 'The struggle to the top is itself enough to fill a man's heart. One must imagine Sisyphus happy.' Even in a state of utter hopelessness, Sisyphus can still be happy. Indeed, he is happy precisely *because* he is in a state of utter hopelessness: because in recognizing and accepting its hopelessness, he might at last transcend his condition.

We can have hopes, indeed, we have to have hopes; but we also have to have insight into our hopes, and into the process and nature of hoping. Else we may take ourselves too seriously and suffer for it.

15

Nostalgia

By the rivers of Babylon, there we sat down,
yea, we wept, when we remembered Zion.

—Psalm 137

Nostalgia is sentimentality for the past, typically for a particular period or place with positive associations, but sometimes also for the past in general, 'the good old days' of yore. At the end of André Brink's novel, *An Instant in the Wind*, the character of Adam memorably says, 'The land which happened inside us no one can take away from us again, not even ourselves.' Nostalgia combines the sadness of loss with the joy or satisfaction that the loss is not complete, nor ever can be. Mortal though we are, whatever little life we have snared from the legions of death is forever ours.

'Nostalgia' is a portmanteau neologism coined in 1688 by Swiss medical student Johannes Hofer from the Greek *nóstos* (home-coming) and *álgos* (pain, ache). *Nóstos* is, of course, the overriding theme of Homer's *Odyssey*, in which Odysseus strives to return to Penelope and Telemachus and his native Ithaca in the aftermath of the Trojan War. In Virgil's *Aeneid*, Aeneas, another survivor of the

Trojan War and the ancestor of Romulus and Remus, gazes upon a Carthaginian mural depicting battles of the Trojan War and the deaths of his kin. Moved to tears, he cries out, *sunt lacrimae rerum et mentem mortalia tangunt*: 'These are the tears of things and mortal things touch the mind.'

Hofer coined 'nostalgia' to refer to the homesickness of Swiss mercenaries fighting in foreign lowlands. Military physicians attributed this homesickness, also known as *Schweizerheimweh* or *mal du suisse*, to ear and brain damage from the constant clanging of cowbells. Recognized symptoms included pining for Alpine landscapes, fainting, fever, and even, *in extremis*, death. In the *Dictionnaire de musique*, Rousseau claims that Swiss mercenaries were forbidden from singing their Swiss songs so as not to exacerbate their nostalgia. By the 19th century, nostalgia had become a topos in Romantic literature, inspiring a fashion for alpinism among the European cultural elite.

Today, nostalgia is no longer looked upon as a mental disorder, but as a natural, common, and even positive emotion, a vehicle for travelling beyond the deadening confines of time and space. Bouts of nostalgia are often prompted by feelings of loneliness, disconnectedness, or meaninglessness; thoughts about the past; particular places and objects; and smell, touch, music, and weather. When I was a child, I kept a lock of fur from my English sheepdog Oscar after he got run over by a tractor and had to be put down. Like the toys and books of our childhood, or our childhood home, the lock became a sort of time portal, which, for many years, helped me to nostalgize about Oscar. I say 'help' because nostalgia does have an unexpected number of adaptive functions. Our everyday is humdrum, often even absurd. Nostalgia can lend us much-needed context, perspective, and direction, reminding and reassuring us that our life (and that of others) is not as banal as it may seem, that it is rooted in a narrative, and that there have been—and will once again be—meaningful moments and experiences. In that much, nostalgia serves a similar function to anticipation, which can be defined as enthusiasm and excitement for some expected or hoped-for positive event. The hauntings of times gone by, and the imaginings of times to come, strengthen us in lesser times.

It is a strange thing: a vivid memory from the distant past, haunted by people who have grown up or grown old or are no more, doing things that are no longer done in a world that no longer exists. And yet it all seems so vivid in our minds that we can still picture the glint in their eye or the twitch in the corner of their mouth. Sometimes we even say their names under our breath as if that could magically bring them back to us. Nostalgia is nothing if not paradoxical. In supplying us with substance and texture, it also reminds us of their lack, moving us to restoration. Unfortunately, this restoration often takes the form of spending, and marketers rely on nostalgia to sell us everything from music and clothes to cars and houses. Many of our social connections endure solely or mostly out of nostalgia, so much so that inducing or sharing in a nostalgic moment can at once revive a flagging relationship. Nostalgia is more frequent in uncertain times and times of transition or change. According to one study, it is also commoner on cold days or in cold rooms, and makes us feel warmer!

On the other hand, it could be argued that nostalgia is a form of self-deception in that it invariably involves distortion and idealization of the past, not least because the bad or boring bits fade from memory more quickly than the peak experiences. The Romans had a tag for the phenomenon that psychologists have come to call 'rosy retrospection': *memoria praeteritorum bonorum*, 'the past is always well remembered'. If overindulged, nostalgia can give rise to a utopia that never existed and can never exist, but that is pursued at all costs, sapping all life and joy and potential from the present. For many people, paradise is not so much a place to go to as the place that they came from.

Nostalgia ought to be distinguished from homesickness and from regret. Although homesickness is a loan translation of nostalgia, it refers more specifically to the distress or impairment caused by an actual or anticipated separation from home. Regret is a conscious negative emotional reaction to past actions or lack thereof. Regret differs from disappointment in that regret is of actions, disappointment of outcomes. Guilt (Chapter 4) is deep regret for actions because they fell short of our own moral standards. Guilt is a prerequisite for remorse, which is more mature and proactive than guilt in that it also involves an impulse for repentance and reparation.

Nostalgia can more fruitfully be compared with a number of similar or related concepts including *saudade*, *mono no aware*, *wabi-sabi*, *dukkha*, and *Sehnsucht*. *Saudade* is a Portuguese and Galician word for the love and longing for someone or something that has been lost and may never be regained. It is the desolate incompleteness or wistful dreaminess that can be felt even in the presence of its object, when that presence is threatened or incomplete—as, for example, in the famous final scene of *Cinema Paradiso*. The rise of *saudade* coincided with the decline of Portugal and the yen for its imperial heyday, a yen so strong as to have written itself into the national anthem: *Levantai hoje de novo o splendor de Portugal* ('Let us once again lift up the splendor of Portugal').

The literal translation of the Japanese *mono no aware* is 'the pathos of things'. Coined in the 18th century by Motoori Norinaga for his literary criticism of the *Tale of Genjii*, it refers to a heightened consciousness of the transience of things coupled with an acute appreciation of their ephemeral beauty and a gentle sadness or wistfulness at their passing—and, by extension, at the realization, reminder, or truth that all things must pass. Although beauty itself is eternal in its recurrence, its particular manifestations are unique and special because they cannot in themselves be either preserved or recreated.

Related to *mono no aware* is *wabi-sabi*, an aesthetic of impermanence and imperfection rooted in Zen Buddhism. *Wabi-sabi* calls upon the acceptance and espousal of transience and inadequacy to foster a sense of serene melancholy and spiritual longing, and, with it, liberation from the material and mundane distractions of the everyday. Hagi pots with their pockmarked surfaces, cracked glaze, and signature chip are an embodiment of *wabi-sabi*. With age, the pots take on deeper tones and become even more fragile and unique. Haiku poems* that evoke transience and loneliness are another paradigm of *wabi sabi*. Here is a pair of haikus that I wrote in Mauritius.

The sunlit seabed—
A golden reticulum
Of racing ribbons.

The moonlit lagoon—
Silver scales scintillating
On quivering brine.

---

* Traditional Haikus take nature as their subject, and take the form of 17 morae in three phrases of 5, 7, and 5 morae.

The Buddha is reputed to have said, "I have taught one thing and one thing only, *dukkha* and the cessation of *dukkha*." That *dukkha*, or 'suffering', is inherent in all life is the first of the Four Noble Truths of Buddhism. The second Noble Truth is that the cause of all suffering is lust in the extended sense of coveting or craving. The deepest form of *dukkha* is the feeling of dissatisfaction that things, being impermanent and insubstantial, can never measure up to our standards or expectations. Once we have grasped this truth, we stop craving and struggling in hope and fear, and open ourselves up to the ways of the world. We still suffer, but the sting in our suffering has been removed because we understand that, for want of better words, our dissatisfaction has little to do with us as independent agents.

Sehnsucht is German for 'longing' or 'craving'. It is dissatisfaction with an imperfect reality paired with the conscious or unconscious yearning for an ideal that comes to seem more real than the reality itself, as in the final lines of Walt Whitman's *Song of the Universal*:

> *Is it a dream?*
> *Nay, but the lack of it the dream,*
> *And, failing it, life's lore and wealth a dream,*
> *And all the world a dream.*

CS Lewis called *Sehnsucht* 'the inconsolable longing' in the human heart for 'we know not what'. In *The Pilgrim's Regress*, he describes the feeling as 'that unnameable something, desire for which pierces us like a rapier at the smell of bonfire, the sound of wild ducks flying overhead, the title of *The Well at the World's End*, the opening lines of *Kubla Khan*, the morning cobwebs in late summer, or the noise of falling waves.'

Lewis redefines this feeling as 'joy', which he understands as 'an unsatisfied desire which is itself more desirable than any other satisfaction', and which I sometimes think of—in the broadest sense—as our aesthetic and creative reservoir. The paradox of 'joy' arises from the self-defeating nature of human desire, which might be thought of as nothing more or less than a desire for desire, a longing for longing. In *The Weight of Glory*, Lewis illustrates this from the age-old quest for beauty:

> *The books or the music in which we thought the beauty was located will betray us if we trust to them; it was not in them, it only came through them, and what came through them was longing. These things—the beauty, the memory of our own past—are good images of what we really desire; but if they are mistaken for the thing itself they turn into dumb idols, breaking the hearts of their worshippers. For they are not the thing itself; they are only the scent of a flower we have not found, the echo of a tune we have not heard, news from a country we have not visited.*

16

Ambition

A man's worth is no greater than
the worth of his ambitions.

—Marcus Aurelius

Ambition derives from the Latin *ambitio*, 'a going around (to solicit votes)', and, by extension, 'a striving for honour, recognition, and preferment'. It can be defined as a striving for some kind of achievement or distinction, and involves, first, the desire for achievement, and, second, the motivation and determination to strive for its attainment even in the face of adversity and failure. To be ambitious is to achieve first and foremost not for the sake of achievement itself (which is to be high-reaching) but for the sake of distinguishing ourselves from other people. Were we the last person on earth, to be ambitious would make little or no sense.

There are a number of variant concepts or definitions of ambition. For instance, in his *Ethics*, Spinoza remarks that 'everyone endeavours as much as possible to make others love what he loves, and to hate what he hates':

This effort to make everyone approve what we love or hate is in truth ambition, and so we see that each person by nature desires that other persons should live according to his way of thinking...

Ambition is often confused with aspiration. Unlike mere aspiration, which has a particular goal for object, ambition is a trait or disposition, and, as such, is persistent and pervasive. A person cannot alter his ambition any more than he can alter any other character trait: having achieved one goal, the truly ambitious person soon formulates another for which to keep on striving.

Ambition is often spoken of in the same breath as hope (Chapter 14), as in 'hopes and ambitions'. Hope is the desire for something to happen combined with an anticipation of it happening. In contrast, ambition is the desire for achievement or distinction combined with the willingness to strive for its achievement. Generally speaking, ambition is more self-referential and more self-reliant than hope. The opposite of hope is fear, hopelessness, or despair; the opposite of ambition is simply lack of ambition, which is not in itself a negative state.

Ambition is sometimes thought of as a form of greed (Chapter 10), or the acceptable face of greed, which can be defined as the excessive desire for more than is needed or deserved, not for the greater good but for one's own selfish interest. Greed reduces our focus to the pursuit of its object. Ambition, in contrast, is more flexible and far-reaching, and can enable us to flourish and contribute to the flourishing of others. Ultimately, the difference between greed and ambition may simply be one of emphasis, with greed being reductive and destructive, and ambition expansive and adaptive.

In Eastern traditions, ambition is seen as an evil that, by tying us to worldly pursuits, restrains us from the spiritual life and its fruits of virtue, wisdom, and tranquillity. In contrast, in the West, ambition is lauded as a precondition or precursor of success, although the Western canon tends to fall against it. For instance, in the *Republic*, Plato contends that good men care so little for avarice or ambition that they would only be willing to rule if they were to be punished for refusing.

Aristotle had a more nuanced take on ambition. In the *Nicomachean Ethics*, he defines virtue as a disposition to aim at the intermediate, or mean, between excess and deficiency, which, unlike the excess or the deficiency, is a form of success and worthy of praise. For example, he who runs headlong into every danger is rash, and he who flees from every situation is a coward, but courage (Chapter 27) is indicated by the mean. While it is possible to fail in many ways, says Aristotle, it is possible to succeed in one way only, which is why failing is easy and success difficult. By the same token, men may be bad in many ways, but good in one way only.

> *For in everything it is no easy task to find the middle ... anyone can get angry—that is easy—or give or spend money; but to do this to the right person, to the right extent, at the right time, with the right motive, and in the right way, that is not for everyone, nor is it easy; wherefore goodness is both rare and laudable and noble.*

Aristotle proceeds to name and dissect the principal virtues together with their associated vices. In the sphere of 'minor honour and dishonour', he names 'proper ambition' as the virtuous mean, 'ambition' as the vicious excess, and 'lack of ambition' as the vicious deficiency. To this day, people still speak of ambition after Aristotle, as 'healthy ambition', 'unhealthy ambition', and lack of ambition. Healthy ambition can be understood as the measured striving for achievement or distinction, and unhealthy ambition as the immoderate or disordered striving for such. Healthy ambition is life-enhancing, but unhealthy ambition is reductive and destructive and more akin to greed.

In the *Politics*, Aristotle contends that men's avarice and ambition are among the most frequent causes of deliberate acts of injustice. Several centuries later, Francis Bacon refined this proposition: as long as ambitious men go unchecked, they are busy rather than dangerous; but if they are held back, they 'become secretly discontent, and look upon men and matters with an evil eye, and are best pleased, when things go backward'. Bacon advised princes to be cautious in employing ambitious people, and to handle them 'so as they be still progressive and not retrograde'.

Highly ambitious people are sensitive to resistance and failure, and experience an almost constant dissatisfaction or frustration. As with Sisyphus, their task is never finished, and, as with Tantalus, the water than can slake their thirst is always in sight but always out of reach. Just as Tantalus had a rock dangling over his head for all eternity, so ambitious people live with the noose of failure hanging about their necks. Indeed, it is the fear of failure that checks the ambition of all but the most courageous, or rash, of people. Just as mania can end in depression, so ambition can end in anguish and despair. To live with ambition is to live in fear and anxiety, unless, that is, the weight of our ambition can be relieved by gratitude (Chapter 8), which is the feeling of appreciation for past and present goods. Although gratitude is especially lacking in future-focused people, ambition is much less toxic if even without it life can still seem worth living.

A person is not truly ambitious unless he is willing to make sacrifices in the name of his ambition—even though the end of his ambition may not be worth his sacrifices, and not only because it may never be reached or even approached. Indeed, the argument could be made that with pure ambition, the end is never worth the sacrifice. Happily, ambition is rarely pure but usually intermixed with unselfish aims and motives, even if these may be more incidental than deliberate and determining; and it may be that man's greatest achievements are all, or almost all, accidents of ambition. Thus, ambition may be akin to the dangled carrot that goads the donkey and pulls the cart. Studies have found that, on average, ambitious people attain higher levels of education and income, build more prestigious careers, and, despite the nocuous effects of their ambition, report higher levels of overall life satisfaction. Owing to chance and foolishness, most ambitious people end up falling short of their ambitions, but that still lands them far ahead of their more unassuming peers.

In the *Rhetoric*, Aristotle asserts that the effect of good birth, that is, ancestral distinction, is to make people more ambitious. He does however caution that to be wellborn is not to be noble, and that most of the wellborn are wretches nonetheless.

> *In the generations of men as in the fruits of the earth, there is a varying yield; now and then, where the stock is good, exceptional men are produced for a while, and then decadence sets in.*

Both nature and nurture play a role in the development of ambition. For instance, in a family of several children, the youngest child compares himself to his older siblings, and, falling short, might become highly competitive and ambitious, or, conversely, withdraw in the belief that he is fundamentally inadequate. From a purely psycho-logical perspective, ambition can be thought of as an ego defence, which, like all ego defences, serves to protect and uphold a certain notion of the self. Rather than respond with ambition, a person who lacks the strength and courage to take responsibility for his actions is likely to respond with less mature ego defences, for instance, by rationalizing that 'life is unfair' or that he is 'less of a star and more of a team-player'. If his ego is much bigger than his courage, the person might become dismissive or even destructive, the latter also being a means of attracting attention and sabotaging himself so as to furnish a concrete excuse for his failure. In brief, ambition is a complex construct born out of a host of factors including but not limited to parental role models, intelligence, past achievement, fear of failure or rejection, envy, anger, revenge, feelings of inferiority or superior-ity, competitiveness, and the instinctual drives for life and sex.

One ego defence that merits particular exploration in this context is sublimation, which is among the most mature and successful of all ego defences. If a person is angry with his boss, he might go home and kick the dog, or he might instead go out for a run in the park. The first instance (kicking the dog) is an example of displacement, the redirection of uncomfortable feelings towards someone or something less important, which is an immature ego defence. The second instance (going out for a run) is an example of sublimation, the channelling of uncomfortable feelings into socially condoned and often productive activities, which is, of course, a much more mature ego defence.

An example of sublimation pertinent to ambition is the person with sadistic or homicidal urges who provides an outlet for these urges by joining the army or, like Justice Wargrave in Agatha Christie's novel

And Then There Were None, becoming a judge. At the end of the novel, in the postscript, a letter is found in a bottle just off the Devon coast. The letter contains the confession of the late Justice Wargrave, in which he reveals a lifelong sadistic temperament juxtaposed with a fierce sense of justice. Although he longed to terrify, torture, and kill, he could not justify harming innocent people. So instead he became a 'hanging judge' who thrilled at the sight of convicted (and guilty) criminals trembling with fear.

Another example of sublimation pertinent to ambition is that of Gustav von Aschenbach, the middle-aged protagonist of Thomas Mann's novella *Death in Venice*. Aschenbach, who is the alter ego of Mann, is a famous writer suffering from writer's block. While staying at the *Grand Hôtel des Bains* on Venice's Lido Island, he is taken by the sight of a beautiful adolescent boy called Tadzio who is staying at the hotel with his aristocratic family. Aschenbach becomes more and more obsessed with Tadzio, even though he never talks to him and still less touches him. Instead, he sublimes his longing, which he eventually recognizes as sexual, into his writing. Thus, in Chapter 4:

> ... *he, in full sight of his idol and under his canvas, worked on his little treatise – those one-and-a-half pages of exquisite prose, the honesty, nobility and emotional deepness of which caused it to be much admired within a short time. It is probably better that the world knows only the result, not the conditions under which it was achieved; because knowledge of the artist's sources of inspiration might bewilder them, drive them away and in that way nullify the effect of the excellent work.*

In life, few things are either good or bad. Rather, their good and bad depend on what we can or cannot make of them. People with a high degree of healthy ambition are those with the insight and strength (strength that is often born of insight) to control the blind forces of ambition, that is, to shape their ambition so that it matches their interests and ideals, and to harness it so that it fires them without also burning them or those around them.

A person shrinks or expands into the degree and nature of his ambitions. Ambition needs to be cultivated and refined, and yet has no teachers.

17

Anger

In the beginning the Universe was created.
This has made a lot of people very angry and
been widely regarded as a bad move.

—Douglas Adams

Anger is perhaps best defined or understood negatively, by comparing and contrasting it with overlapping emotions such as resentment, contempt, irritability, hatred, and loathing.

Resentment, or bitterness, is an unpleasant emotion, often involving anger, arising from a real or perceived injustice. If it involves someone close or trusted, it is typically complicated and intensified by a feeling of betrayal. People are said to express anger but to *harbour* resentment. Anger is an acute response to a concrete or symbolic threat, and aims to avert or defuse that threat. In contrast, resentment is more chronic or long-term and largely internalized. Even so, resentment can give rise to retaliatory action, sometimes violent but often of a subtler nature than that born of anger.

Contempt is often described as a combination of anger and disgust, and can be either hot or cold. The cardinal feature of contempt is the denial or rejection of a particular claim to respect or standing on the grounds that it is unjustified, often because the person making the claim has violated some norm or expectation and thereby compromised himself. Thus understood, contempt is an attempt at invalidating the claims of its object, and, in so doing, reinforcing those of its subject. Philosopher Robert C. Solomon has argued that contempt is directed at those of a lower status, resentment at those of a higher status, and anger at those of a similar status. If this is correct, the flattening of social structures should lead to a rise in anger and a corresponding fall in contempt and resentment.

Irritability is simply a propensity to anger or annoyance. Hatred is an intense or passionate dislike often arising from anger or fear. Loathing is similar to hatred, but with an emphasis on disgust or intolerance. In *Instinct and their Vicissitudes*, Freud contends that hatred seeks the destruction of its object.

In the 35 dialogues ascribed to him, Plato does not discuss anger in any depth and tends to bring it up only in the context of pleasure and pain. In the *Philebus*, he holds that good people delight in true or good pleasures whereas bad people delight in false or bad pleasures, and that the same is also true of pain, fear, anger, and the like—implying that there can be such a thing as true or good anger. Later on, he maintains that pleasures of the mind may be mixed with pain, as in anger or envy or love, or the mixed feelings of the spectator of tragedy or of the greater drama of life—this time implying that anger can be pleasurable at the same time as it is painful. In the *Timaeus*, he lists five terrible affections of the mortal soul: pleasure, the inciter of evil; pain, which deters from good; rashness and fear, foolish counsellors; anger, hard to appease; and hope, easily led astray. The gods, he says, mingled these affections with irrational sense and all-daring love, and thereby created man.

Unlike Plato, Aristotle discusses anger in great detail. In the *Nicomachean Ethics*, he appears to agree with Plato, advancing that a good-tempered person can sometimes get angry, but only as he ought to. A good-tempered person might get angry too soon or not enough, yet still be praised for being good-tempered. It is only if he deviates more markedly from the mean with respect to anger that he becomes blameworthy, either 'irascible' at one extreme or 'lacking in spirit' at the other. Aristotle also agrees that anger involves mixed feelings of pleasure and pain. In the *Rhetoric*, he defines anger as an impulse, accompanied by pain, to a conspicuous revenge for a conspicuous slight that has been directed at the subject or at his friends. But he adds that anger is also attended by a certain pleasure that arises from the expectation of revenge.

According to Aristotle, a person is slighted out of one of three things: contempt, spite, and insolence. In each case, the slight betrays the offender's feeling that the slighted person is obviously of no importance. The slighted person may or may not be angered, but is more likely to be angered if he is in distress (for example, in poverty or in love) or if he is insecure about the subject of the slight. On the other hand, he is less likely to be angered if the slight is involuntary, unintentional, or itself provoked by anger, or if the offender apologizes or humbles himself before him and behaves as his inferior. He is also less likely to get angry if the offender has done him more kindnesses than he has returned, or reverences him, or is feared and respected by him. Once provoked, anger can be quelled by: the feeling that the slight is deserved, the passage of time, the exaction of revenge, or the suffering of the offender. Alternatively, it can be exhausted on some third party. Thus, although angrier at Ergophilius than at Callisthenes, the people acquitted Ergophilius because they had already condemned Callisthenes to death.

There is clearly a sense in which Plato and Aristotle are justified in speaking of such a thing as good or right anger. Anger can serve a number of useful, even vital, functions. It can put an end to a physical, psychological, or social threat, or, failing that, mobilize mental and bodily resources for aversive, defensive, or retaliatory action. If judiciously exercised, anger can enable a person to signal high social status, compete for rank and position, strengthen bargaining positions, ensure that contracts and promises are fulfilled, and even inspire desirable feelings such as respect and sympathy. A person who is able to express or exercise right anger is likely to feel better about himself, more in control, more optimistic, and more prone to the sort of risk-taking that maximizes outcomes. On the other hand, anger, and especially uncontrolled anger, can lead to loss of perspective and judgement, impulsive and irrational behaviour, and loss of face, sympathy, and social status.

Thus, it appears that the sort of anger that is justified, controlled, strategic, and potentially adaptive ought to be distinguished from and contrasted with a second type of anger—let us call it 'rage'—that is inappropriate, unjustified, unprocessed, irrational, undifferentiated, and uncontrolled. The function of rage is simply to protect the ego. It causes pain of one kind to detract from pain of another, and, unlike right anger, is not associated with pleasure.

Another, related, idea is this. Anger, and particularly rage, strengthens correspondence bias, that is, the tendency to attribute observed behaviours to dispositional factors rather than situational factors. For instance, if I am being a boor, it is because I am having a bad day (situational factor); but if Charles is being a boor, it is because he *is* a boor (dispositional factor). More fundamentally, anger reinforces the illusion that people, being 'at fault', exercise a high degree of free will, whereas in actual fact most of our actions and the neurological activity that they correspond to are determined by past events and the cumulative effects of those past events on our patterns of thinking. Charles is Charles because he is Charles, and, at least in the short-term, there is precious little he can do about that. It follows that the only person who can truly deserve our anger is the one who acted freely, that is, the one who spited us freely and therefore probably rightly!

This does not mean that anger is not justified in other cases, as a display of controlled anger—even if undeserved—can still serve a benevolent strategic purpose, as when we 'get angry' at a child for the benefit of shaping his character. But if all that is ever required is a strategic display of anger, then true anger that involves real pain is entirely superfluous, its presence serving only to betray a certain lack of understanding.

18

Patience

Patience makes lighter what sorrow may not heal.

—Horace

Patience (forbearance) derives from the Latin *patientia*, 'patience, endurance, submission', and, ultimately—like 'passivity' and 'passion'—from *patere*, 'to suffer'. It can be defined as the quality of endurance and equanimity in the face of adversity, from simple delay or provocation to tragic misfortune and mortal pain. Being both beneficial and difficult, patience is often thought of as a virtue, but it can equally be understood as a complex of virtues including self-control, humility, tolerance, generosity, and mercy, and also underlies several other virtues such as hope, faith, and love. It is thus a paradigm for the unity of the virtues.

The Book of Proverbs tells us that, 'he that is slow to anger is better than the mighty; and he that ruleth his spirit than he that taketh a city', and also that, 'by long forbearing is a prince persuaded, and a soft tongue breaketh the bone'. According to Ecclesiastes, 'better is the end of a thing than the beginning thereof: and the patient in spirit is better than the proud in spirit. Be not hasty in thy spirit to be angry: for anger resteth in the bosom of fools.' In Buddhism, patience is named as one of the 'perfections' (*paramitas*), and, as in other religious traditions, extends to the non-return of harm. Thus, Paul's First Epistle to the Thessalonians exhorts, 'be patient toward all men. See that none render evil for evil unto any man; but ever follow that which is good, both among yourselves, and to all men.'

The opposite of patience is, of course, impatience, but also hastiness, impetuosity, and perhaps even cowardice, suggesting that patience may have much in common with courage. Impatience may be defined as the inability or disinclination to endure perceived imperfection. It is a rejection of the present moment on the grounds that it is marred and ought to be supplanted by some more ideal imagined future. Ultimately, impatience amounts to a rejection of the nature of reality. Patience recognizes that life is a struggle for each and every one of us, but impatience takes offense at people for being the kind of people that they are, betraying a certain disregard, even contempt, for human nature in its finitude. Impatience implies impotence, which, in turn, implies frustration, a term that derives from the Latin *frustra*, 'in vain, in error', and is related to *fraus*, 'injury, harm'. Impatience and frustration are as misguided as they are miserable, and as sterile as they are self-defeating. They underlie not only rash and destructive action, but also, paradoxically, procrastination (Chapter 3), since to put off a difficult or boring task is also to put off the irritation and frustration to which it is bound to give rise.

Today more than ever patience is a forgotten virtue. Our individualistic and materialistic society values ambition and action (or, at least, activity) above all else, whereas patience seems to involve a withdrawing and withholding of the self. Technological progress is not helping. In a recent study of millions of internet users, researchers found that, within just 10 seconds, about half of users had given up on videos that had not started to play. Users with a faster connection were fastest to click away, suggesting that superior technology and technological progress is eroding our patience. Waiting, even for a very short time, has become so unbearable to us that much of our economy is geared at eliminating 'dead time'. In *The Art of Failure*, I argued that such restless impatience is an expression of the manic defence, the essence of which is to prevent feelings of helplessness and despair from entering the conscious mind by occupying it with opposite feelings of euphoria, purposeful activity, and omnipotent control.

Even in pre-technological times, the so-called egocentric predicament made patience difficult to exercise. Simply put, because I have privileged access to my own thoughts and feelings, I blow them out of all proportion. If I am impatient in the checkout queue, it is in large part because I am under the impression that my time is more valuable, and my purpose more worthwhile, than that of the mugs standing in front of me. Believing that I could be doing a much better job of operating the till, I give dagger eyes to the cashier, failing to recognize that she is coming at it from a different perspective and with different skills and abilities. In the end, my frustration in itself becomes a source of frustration as I vacillate between biding my time and taking abortive action.

Patience can be regarded as a decision-making problem: eat up all the grain today or plant it in the earth and wait for it to multiply. Unfortunately, human beings evolved not as farmers but as hunter-gatherers, and have a strong tendency to discount long-term rewards. Our ancestral shortsightedness is borne out by the

Stanford marshmallow experiment, a series of studies on delayed gratification led by Walter Mischel in the late 1960s and early 1970s. These studies, conducted on hundreds of mostly four- and five-year old children, involved a simple binary choice: either eat this marshmallow, or hold back for 15 minutes and be given a second marshmallow. Having explained this choice to a child, the experimenter left him alone with the marshmallow for 15 minutes. Follow-up studies carried out over 40 years found that the minority of children who had been able to hold out for a second marshmallow went on to enjoy significantly better life outcomes, including higher test scores, better social skills, and less substance misuse.

Even so, patience involves much more than the mere ability to hold back for some future gain. Exercising patience (note the use of the verb 'to exercise') can be compared to dieting or growing a garden. Yes, waiting is involved, but one also needs to have a plan in place, and, moreover, to work at that plan. Thus, when it comes to others, patience does not amount to mere restraint or toleration, but to a complicit engagement in their struggle and welfare. In that much, patience is a form of compassion, which, rather than disregarding and alienating people, turns them into friends and allies.

If impatience implies impotence, patience implies power, power born out of understanding. Rather than make us into a hostage to fortune, patience frees us from frustration and its ills, delivers us to the present moment, and affords us the calm and perspective to think, say, and do the right thing in the right way at the right time— which is why, with psychotherapy, both patient and therapist can require several years together. Last but not least, patience enables us to achieve things that would otherwise have been impossible to achieve. As La Bruyère put it, 'There is no road too long to the man who advances deliberately and without undue haste; there are no honours too distant to the man who prepares himself for them with patience.' Exercising patience does not mean never protesting or giving up, but only ever doing so in a considered fashion: never impetuously, never pettily, and never pointlessly. Neither does it mean withholding, just like ageing a case of fine wine for several years does not mean withholding from wine during all that time. Life is too short to wait, but it is not too short for patience.

Patience is much easier, perhaps even pleasant, to exercise if one truly understands that it can and does deliver much better outcomes, not just for ourselves but for others too. In 2012, researchers at the University of Rochester replicated the marshmallow experiment. However, before doing so, they split the participating children into two groups, exposing one group to unreliable experiences in the form of broken promises, and the other to reliable experiences in the form of honoured promises. They subsequently found that the children exposed to honoured promises waited an average of *four times longer* than the children exposed to broken promises.

In other words, patience is largely a matter of trust, or, some might say, faith.

19

Depression

Grief is the price we pay for love.

—Elizabeth II of the United Kingdom

Today sadness, particularly if intense or prolonged, is typically thought of in terms of depression, that is, a biological illness of the brain. Here I argue, as I have in *The Meaning of Madness*, that the concept of depression as a mental disorder has been unhelpfully overextended to include all manner of human suffering, and, more controversially, that 'depression' can actually be good for us.

Let us begin by thinking very broadly about the concept of depression. There are important geographical variations in the prevalence of depression, and these can in large part be accounted for by socio-cultural rather than biological factors. In traditional societies, emotional distress is more likely to be interpreted as an indicator of the need to address important life problems rather than as a mental disorder requiring professional treatment, and so a diagnosis of depression is correspondingly less common. Some linguistic communities do not even have a word for 'depression', and many people from traditional societies with what may be construed as depression present instead with physical complaints such as fatigue, headache, or chest pain. Punjabi women who have recently immigrated to the UK and given birth find it baffling that a health visitor should pop round to ask them if they are depressed, not least because they had never considered that giving birth could be anything other than a joyous event.

In modern societies such as the UK and the USA, people are encouraged to talk about depression and do so more readily and easily. As a result, they are more likely to interpret their distress in terms of depression and to seek out a diagnosis of the illness. At the same time, groups with vested interests such as pharmaceutical companies and so-called mental health experts actively promote the notion of saccharine happiness as a natural, default state, and of human distress as a mental disorder. The concept of depression as a mental disorder may be useful for the more severe and intractable cases treated by hospital psychiatrists, but not for the majority of cases, which, for the most part, are mild and short-lived and easily interpreted in terms of life circumstances, human nature, or the human condition.

Another non-mutually exclusive explanation for the important geographical variations in the prevalence of depression may lie in the nature of modern societies, which have become increasingly individualistic and divorced from traditional values. For many people living in our society, life can seem both suffocating and far removed, lonely even and especially among the multitudes, and not only meaningless but absurd. By encoding their distress in terms of a mental disorder, our society is subtly implying that the problem lies not with itself but with them, fragile and failing individuals that they are. Of course, many people prefer to buy into this reductive explanation than to confront their existential angst. But thinking of unhappiness in terms of an illness or chemical imbalance can be counterproductive because it can prevent us from identifying and addressing the important psychological or life problems that are at the root of our distress.

All this is not to say that the concept of depression as a mental disorder is bogus, but merely that the diagnosis of depression has been over-extended to include far more than just depression the mental disorder. If, like the majority of medical conditions, depression could be defined and diagnosed according to its aetiology or pathology—that is, according to its physical cause or effect—such a state of affairs could never have arisen. Unfortunately, depression cannot as yet be defined according to its aetiology or pathology, but only according to its clinical manifestations and symptoms. This means that a physician cannot base a diagnosis of depression on any objective criterion such as a blood test or a brain scan, but only on his subjective interpretation of the nature and severity of the patient's symptoms. If some of these symptoms appear to tally with the very loose diagnostic criteria for depression, then the physician is able to justify a diagnosis of depression.

One important problem here is that the definition of 'depression' is circular: the concept of depression is defined according to the symptoms of depression, which are in turn defined according to the concept of depression. For this reason, it is impossible to be certain that the concept of depression maps onto any distinct disease entity, particularly since a diagnosis of depression can apply to anything from mild depression to depressive psychosis and depressive stupor, and overlap with several other categories of mental disorder including dysthymia, adjustment disorders, and anxiety disorders.

141

One of the consequences of our 'menu of symptoms' approach to diagnosing depression is that two people with absolutely no symptoms in common can both end up with the same block diagnosis of depression. For this reason especially, the concept of depression as a mental disorder has been charged with being little more than a socially constructed dustbin for all manner of human suffering.

Let us grant, as the orthodoxy has it, that every person inherits a certain complement of genes that makes him more or less vulnerable to entering a state that could be diagnosed as depression (and let us also refer to this state as 'the depressive position' to include the entire continuum of depressed mood, including but not limited to clinical depression). A person enters the depressive position if the amount of stress that he comes under is greater than the amount of stress that he can tolerate given the complement of genes that he has inherited. Genes for potentially debilitating disorders gradually pass out of a population over time because affected people have, on average, fewer children or fewer healthy children than non-affected people. But the fact that this has not happened for depression suggests that the genes responsible are being maintained despite their potentially debilitating effects on a significant proportion of the population, and thus that they are conferring an important adaptive advantage.

There are other instances of genes that both predispose to an illness and confer an important adaptive advantage. In sickle cell disease, for example, red blood cells assume a rigid sickle shape that restricts their passage through tiny blood vessels. This leads to a number of serious physical complications, and in the absence of modern medicine, to a radically curtailed life expectancy. At the same time, carrying just one allele of the sickle cell gene ('sickle cell trait') makes it impossible for malarial parasites to reproduce inside red blood cells, and thereby confers immunity to malaria. The fact that the gene for sickle cell disease is commonest in populations from malarial regions suggests that, at least in evolutionary terms, a debilitating illness in a few can be a price worth paying for an important advantage in the many.

What important adaptive advantage could the depressive position be conferring? Just as physical pain has evolved to signal injury and prevent further injury, so the depressive position evolved to remove us from distressing, damaging, or futile situations. The time and space and solitude that the depressive position affords prevent us from making rash decisions, enable us to reconnect with the bigger picture, and encourage us to reassess our social relationships, think about those who matter most to us, and relate to them more meaningfully and with greater compassion. In other words, the depressive position evolved as a signal that something is seriously wrong and needs working through and changing, or, at the very least, processing and understanding.

Sometimes we can become so immersed in the humdrum of our everyday lives that we no longer have the time to think and feel about ourselves, and so lose sight of our bigger picture. The adoption of the depressive position can force us to cast off the polyannish optimism and rose-tinted spectacles that shield us from reality, stand back at a distance, re-evaluate and prioritize our needs, and formulate a modest but realistic plan for fulfilling them.

At an even deeper level, the adoption of the depressive position can lead us to develop a more refined perspective and deeper understanding of ourselves, our lives, and life in general. From an existential standpoint, the adoption of the depressive position obliges us to become aware of our mortality and freedom, and challenges us to exercise the latter within the framework of the former. By meeting this difficult challenge, we are able to break out of the mould that has been imposed upon us, discover who we truly are, and, in so doing, begin to give deep meaning to our lives.

Many of the most creative and insightful people in society have suffered from depression or a state that could be diagnosed as depression. They include the politicians Winston Churchill and Abraham Lincoln; the poets Charles Baudelaire, Elizabeth Bishop, Hart Crane, Emily Dickinson, Sylvia Plath, and Rainer Maria Rilke; the thinkers Michel Foucault, William James, John Stuart Mill, Isaac Newton, Friedrich Nietzsche, and Arthur Schopenhauer; and the writers Agatha Christie, Charles Dickens, William Faulkner, Graham Greene, Leo Tolstoy, Evelyn Waugh, and Tennessee Williams—among many, many others. To quote Marcel Proust, who himself suffered from depression, 'Happiness is good for the body, but it is grief which develops the strengths of the mind.'

People in the depressive position are often stigmatized as 'failures' or 'losers'. Of course, nothing could be further from the truth. If these people are in the depressive position, it is most probably because they have tried too hard or taken on too much, so hard and so much that they have made themselves 'ill with depression'. That is to say, if these people are in the depressive position, it is because their world was simply not good enough for them. They wanted more, they wanted better, and they wanted different, not just for themselves, but for all those around them. So if they are failures or losers, this is only because they set the bar far too high. They could have swept everything under the carpet and pretended, as many people do, that all is for the best in the best of possible worlds. But unlike many people, they had the honesty and the strength to admit that something was amiss, that something was not quite right. So rather than being failures or losers, they are just the opposite: they are ambitious, they are truthful, and they are courageous. And that is precisely why they got 'ill'.

To make them believe that they are suffering from some chemical imbalance in the brain and that their recovery depends solely or even partly upon popping pills is to do them a great disfavour: it is to deny them the precious opportunity not only to identify and address important life problems, but also to develop a deeper and more refined appreciation of themselves and of the world around them—and therefore to deny them the opportunity to fulfil their highest potential as human beings.

20

Fear and anxiety

Anxiety is the dizziness of freedom.

—Kierkegaard

Anxiety can be defined as 'a state consisting of psychological and physical symptoms brought about by a sense of apprehension at a perceived threat'. Fear is similar to anxiety, except that with fear the threat is, or is perceived to be, more concrete, present, or immediate.

Fear and anxiety can be a normal response to life experiences, a protective mechanism that has evolved both to prevent us from entering into potentially dangerous situations and to assist us in escaping from them should they befall us regardless. For instance, fear and anxiety can prevent us from coming into close contact with disease-carrying or poisonous animals such as rats, snakes, and spiders; from engaging with a much stronger or angrier enemy; and even from declaring our undying love to someone who is unlikely to spare our feelings. The fight-or-flight response triggered by fear can help us to confront or escape from a threat by priming our body for action and increasing our performance and stamina. In short, the purpose of fear and anxiety is to preserve us from injury and, above all, from death—whether literal or metaphorical, biological or psychosocial.

At the same time, severe or inappropriate anxiety can be maladaptive, and, in some cases, even prevent us from doing the sorts of things that most people take for granted such as caring for our personal needs or enjoying the companionship of our friends and family. Such pathological anxiety is very common, and often presents in one or more distinct patterns or syndromes such as a specific phobia, panic disorder, or post-traumatic stress disorder (PTSD).

Still, as with adaptive forms of anxiety, each of these pathological forms of anxiety can be interpreted and understood in terms of life and death. Common specific phobias such as arachnophobia (spiders), claustrophobia (enclosed spaces), acrophobia (heights), achluophobia (darkness), brontophobia (storms), and haematophobia (blood) are all for the sorts of dangers that commonly threatened our ancestors. Though man-made hazards such as drunken drivers and electric cables are now far more likely to put us out than natural dangers, most phobias remain for natural dangers, presumably because man-made hazards have not had time to imprint themselves onto our genome.

Panic disorder involves recurrent panic attacks during which symptoms of anxiety are so severe that the person fears that he is suffocating, having a heart attack, losing control, or even 'going crazy'. As a result, he develops a fear of the panic attacks themselves, which in turn sets off further panic attacks. A vicious cycle takes hold, with the panic attacks becoming ever more frequent and severe and even occurring 'out of the blue'.

As with specific phobias, the ulterior fear in panic disorder is of death and dying, as it is also with PTSD, which is a reaction to a traumatic life event such as a bomb shelling, car crash, or rape. Common symptoms of PTSD include anxiety, of course, but also numbing, detachment, flashbacks, nightmares, and partial or complete loss of memory for the traumatic event. The symptoms of PTSD vary significantly from one culture to another, so much so that PTSD is often thought of as a culture-bound syndrome.

Many if not all culture-bound syndromes are essentially culture-specific anxiety disorders, which, like other anxiety disorders, can easily be understood in existential terms. For instance, Koro, seen in South Asian men, involves sudden and intense fear of the penis retracting into the body and causing death. Koro may represent a reaction to sexual guilt, with some men going so far as to fasten their penis to posts or pieces of furniture so as to forestall its deadly retraction. Dhat, also seen in South Asian men, involves sudden fear about loss of semen in the urine, whitish discoloration of the urine, and sexual dysfunction, combined with feelings of weakness and exhaustion. Dhat may be rooted in the Hindu belief that it takes forty drops of blood to create a drop of bone marrow, and forty drops of bone marrow to create a drop of semen, and thus that semen is a concentrated essence of life.

While pathological forms of anxiety such as specific phobias, panic disorder, and PTSD are grounded in threats to life, existential anxiety is rooted in the brevity and apparent absurdity or meaninglessness of life. Existential anxiety is so disturbing that most people avoid it at all costs, constructing a false reality out of habits, customs, values, culture, and religion so as to deceive themselves that their lives are special and meaningful and that death is distant or delusory.

However, such self-deception comes at a heavy price. According to Sartre, people who refuse to face up to 'non-being' are acting in 'bad faith' and living out a life that is inauthentic and unfulfilling. Facing up to non-being can bring insecurity, loneliness, responsibility, and consequently anxiety, but it can also bring a sense of calm, freedom, and even nobility. Far from being pathological, existential anxiety is a sign of health, strength, and courage, and a harbinger of bigger and better things to come.

For theologian Paul Tillich, refusing to face up to non-being leads not only to a life that is inauthentic but also to pathological (or neurotic) anxiety. In *The Courage to Be*, Tillich asserts, 'He who does not succeed in taking his anxiety courageously upon himself can succeed in avoiding the extreme situation of despair by escaping into neurosis. He still affirms himself but on a limited scale. Neurosis is the way of avoiding nonbeing by avoiding being.' According to this outlook, pathological anxiety, though seemingly grounded in threats to life, in fact arises from repressed existential anxiety, which itself arises from our uniquely human capacity for self-consciousness.

By facing up to death and accepting its inevitability, we are able to cure ourselves of pathological anxiety and, for the first time, put our life into perspective, see in in its entirety, and lend it a sense of direction and unity. It is only by integrating death into life that we can escape from the pettiness and paralysis of anxiety, and, in so doing, free ourselves to make the most out of our life and out of ourselves.

Some philosophers have gone even further by asserting that the very purpose of life is none other than to prepare for death. In Plato's *Phaedo*, Socrates, who is not long to die, tells the philosophers Simmias and Cebes that absolute justice, absolute beauty, or absolute good cannot be apprehended with the eyes or any other bodily organ but only by the mind or soul. Therefore, the philosopher seeks in as far as possible to separate body from soul and become pure soul. As death is the complete separation of body and soul, the philosopher aims at death, and indeed can be said to be almost dead.

21

Empathy

To perceive is to suffer.

—Aristotle

In 1909, the psychologist Edward Titchener translated the German *Einfühlung* ('feeling into') into English as 'empathy'. Empathy can be defined as a person's ability to recognize and share the emotions of another person, fictional character, or sentient being. It involves, first, seeing someone else's situation from his perspective, and, second, sharing his emotions, including, if any, his distress.

For me to share in someone else's perspective, I must do more than merely put myself into his position. Instead, I must imagine myself as him, and, more than that, imagine myself as him in the particular situation in which he finds himself. I cannot empathize with an abstract or detached feeling. To empathize with a particular person, I need to have at least some knowledge of who he is and what he is doing or trying to do. As John Steinbeck wrote, 'It means very little to know that a million Chinese are starving unless you know one Chinese who is starving.'

Empathy is often confused with pity, sympathy, and compassion, which are each reactions to the plight of others. Pity is a feeling of discomfort at the distress of one or more sentient beings, and often has paternalistic or condescending overtones. Implicit in the notion of pity is that its object does not deserve its plight, and, moreover, is unable to prevent, reverse, or overturn it. Pity is less engaged than empathy, sympathy, or compassion, amounting to little more than a conscious acknowledgement of the plight of its object.

Sympathy ('fellow feeling', 'community of feeling') is a feeling of care and concern for someone, often someone close, accompanied by a wish to see him better off or happier. Compared to pity, sympathy implies a greater sense of shared similarities together with a more profound personal engagement. However, sympathy, unlike empathy, does not involve a shared perspective or shared emotions, and while the facial expressions of sympathy do convey caring and concern, they do not convey shared distress. Sympathy and empathy often lead to each other, but not in all cases. For instance, it is possible to sympathize with such things as hedgehogs and ladybirds, but not, strictly speaking, to empathize with them. Conversely, psychopaths with absolutely no sympathy for their victims can nonetheless make use of empathy to snare or torture them. Sympathy should also be distinguished from benevolence, which is a much more detached and impartial attitude.

Compassion ('suffering with') is more engaged than simple empathy, and is associated with an active desire to alleviate the suffering of its object. With empathy, I share your emotions; with compassion I not only share your emotions but also elevate them into a universal and transcending experience. Compassion, which builds upon empathy, is one of the main motivators of altruism (Chapter 22).

A friend tearfully confides that her partner is physically abusing her. Moved by her plight, I try to comfort her: "I know just how you feel." To my horror, she is now angry as well as upset: "No, you don't know how I feel! How could you?" Notice that, in claiming that I cannot know how she feels, my friend is also claiming, albeit implicitly, that she can know how I feel—or, at least, that however I feel is not how she feels. But if she is right that I cannot know how she feels, how can she know how I feel, and that how I feel is not how she feels? A similar paradox is raised in the *Zhuangzi*, which is one of the two foundational texts of Taoism:

> *Zhuangzi and Hui Shi were strolling on the bridge above the Hao river. Zhuangzi said, "Out swim the minnows so free and easy, this is the happiness of fish." Hui Shi said, "You are not a fish. Whence do you know the happiness of fish?" Zhuangzi said, "You are not me. Whence do you know I don't know the happiness of fish?" Hui Shi said, "Granted that I am not you, I don't know about you. Then granted that you are not a fish, the case for your not knowing the happiness of fish is complete." Zhuangzi said, "Let's trace back to the root of the issue. When you said, 'Whence do you know the fish are happy?', you asked me already knowing I knew it. I knew it from up above the Hao.*

Empathy rests on theory of mind, which is the ability to understand that other people see things differently from us, and that they have different beliefs, desires, emotions, and so on. Theory of mind is innate ('from up above the Hao'), first appearing at about four years of age. It develops over time, and, for each individual and in general, can be trained in extent and accuracy. It enables us not only to empathize with other people, but also to posit their intentions and predict and explain their behaviour. It has been suggested that the neural basis of theory of mind resides in mirror neurons, which are excited when we carry out a particular action, and also, critically, when we observe that same action in another person. The neurons 'mirror' the actions of the other person such that they become ours, or, rather, as good as ours. This enables us to interpret the actions and infer the kind of state of mind that motivated them. Mirror neuron abnormalities may underlie certain cognitive disorders, most notably autism.

Empathy has been selected for in the course of human evolution because it promotes parental care, social attachment, and prosocial behaviour, and so the survival of the gene pool. It also facilitates social interactions, group operations, and teaching and learning. Although it does involve a degree of identification, it conserves enough distance and detachment for the subject to make moral and normative judgements about the object. This independent perspective can enable the subject to assist the object more effectively than he can assist himself.

On the other hand, empathy can bias us towards its object, leading us to place his interests above those of others and even, in some cases, above justice and the law. Moreover, our capacity for empathy is naturally limited, both in accuracy and capacity. Numerous or repeated demands on our empathy can be exhausting, leading to 'compassion fatigue' and burnout. People who are surrounded by human distress naturally restrict their ability to empathize, not out of callousness or unconcern but from a basic instinct for self-preservation. Fortunately, in less pressured circumstances the exercise of empathy is often rewarding and even revitalizing. A doctor who is able to empathize with his patients, although not so much as to lie awake at night, is much more likely to be fulfilled in his job—to say nothing of the benefit to his patients.

22

Altruism

"What is nobler," she mused, turning over the photographs,
"than to be a woman to whom every one turns,
in sorrow or difficulty?"

—Virginia Woolf

Like empathy, altruism is a modern term, coined in the 19th century by philosopher Auguste Comte from the French *autrui*, which itself derives from the Latin *alteri* ('other people'). It can be defined as the unselfish concern for the welfare of others. The historical notion that most approaches our concept of altruism is almsgiving, a word which derives from the Greek *eleos* ('pity'), and which can be defined as giving to others as an act of charity. In Christian philosophy, charity, which is one of the three theological virtues (Chapter 14), is the love of man for God, and through God, for his fellow men.

Compassion (Chapter 21) is one of the main motivators of altruism. Another, less flattering, motivator for altruism is fear. In such cases, altruism becomes an ego defence, a type of sublimation (Chapter 16) in which a person deals with his problems and anxieties by stepping outside himself and helping others. By focusing on the needs of others, people in altruistic vocations such as medicine, nursing, or teaching may be able to push their own needs into the background where they can more easily be ignored or forgotten. Similarly, people who care for a disabled or elderly person, or even for healthy and independent children, often experience profound anxiety and distress when this role is suddenly removed from them.

Regardless of its motivation, altruism has benefits. In the short-term, carrying out an altruistic act leaves us with a euphoric feeling or so-called 'helpers' high'. In the longer term, altruism is associated with better mental and physical health and greater longevity. Kinder people are happier, and happier people are kinder, giving rise to a virtuous cycle of altruism. At a social level, altruism serves as a signal of cooperative intentions, and also of resource availability and so of mating or partnering potential. It also opens up a debt account, encouraging our beneficiaries to reciprocate with gifts and favours that are potentially of much greater value to us than those with which we felt ready to part. More generally, altruism helps to build and maintain the social fabric that shields, sustains, and enriches us.

In light of all these benefits, many thinkers contend that there can be no such thing as a genuine altruistic act. So-called altruistic acts, they argue, are performed because they lead to pleasant feelings of pride and satisfaction, the expectation of honour or reciprocation, or the greater likelihood of a place in heaven; or, at the very least, because they relieve anxiety or prevent unpleasant feelings such as the guilt or shame of not having acted at all.

The bottom line, I think, is this. There can be no such thing as an altruistic act that does not involve at least some element of self-interest, no such thing, for example, as an altruistic act that does not lead to some degree, no matter how small, of pride or satisfaction. Therefore, an act should not be written off as selfish simply because it includes some unavoidable element of self-interest. The act can still be counted as altruistic if the 'selfish' element is incidental; or if not incidental, then secondary; or if neither incidental nor secondary, then undetermining*.

The real question is: how many so-called altruistic acts can be said to meet these criteria?

---

* 'Undetermining' in that the selfish element did not motivate the act, which would have taken place even in the absence of the selfish element.

23

Friendship

*A man is happy if he has merely encountered
the shadow of a friend.*

—Menander

Plato and Aristotle both give an important place to friendship in the good life: Plato devotes the major part of three books (*Lysis*, *Phaedrus*, and *Symposium*) to friendship and to love, and in Book 8 of the *Nicomachean Ethics* Aristotle lavishes extravagant praise upon the Greek concept of friendship or *philia*, which includes not only voluntary relationships but also those relationships that hold between members of a family. Friendship, says Aristotle, is a virtue which is 'most necessary with a view to living ... for without friends no one would choose to live, though he had all other goods'.

If friendship is an essential ingredient of the good life, then it is important to ask the question, what is friendship? According to Aristotle, for a person to be in friendship with another 'it is necessary that [they] bear good will to each other and wish good things for each other, without this escaping their notice'. A person may bear good will to another for one of three reasons: that he is good (that is, rational and virtuous), that he is pleasant, or that he is useful. While Aristotle leaves room for the idea that relationships based on advantage alone or pleasure alone can give rise to friendships, he believes that such relationships have a smaller claim to being called friendships than those that are based partly or wholly on virtue. 'Now those who wish well to their friends for their sake are most truly friends; for they do this by reason of their own nature and not incidentally; therefore their friendship lasts as long as they are good—and goodness is an enduring thing.' Friendships that are based partly or wholly on virtue are desirable not only because they are associated with a high degree of mutual benefit, but also because they are associated with companionship, dependability, and trust. More important still, to be in such a friendship and to seek out the good of one's friend is to exercise reason and virtue, which is the distinctive function of human beings, and which amounts to happiness.

For Aristotle, an act of friendship is undertaken both for our own good and that of our friend, and there is no reason to think that the one precludes the other. In any case, to have a perfect friend is like having another self, since perfect friends make the same choices as each other and each one's happiness adds to that of the other. Unfortunately, the number of people with whom one can sustain a perfect friendship is very small, first, because reason and virtue are not to be found in everyone (never, for instance, in young people, who are not yet wise enough to be virtuous), and, second, because a perfect friendship can only be created and sustained if a pair of friends spend a great deal of exclusive time together. Thus, even if one lived entirely surrounded by virtuous people, one would only ever have the time for at most a small handful of perfect friends.

Despite his high opinion of friendship, Aristotle is quite clear that the best and happiest life is not that spent in friendship, but that spent in the contemplation of those things that are most true and therefore most beautiful and most dependable. There is a contradiction here: if the best life is one of philosophical contemplation, then friendship is either superfluous or inimical to the best life, and therefore undeserving of the high praise that Aristotle lavishes upon it. It may be, as Aristotle tentatively suggests, that friendship is needed because it leads to contemplation, or that contemplation is only possible some of the time and friendship is needed the rest of the time, or even that a life of friendship is just as good as a life of contemplation.

So much for Aristotle, one might say. Plato also gives an important place to friendship in the good life. He ostensibly devotes an entire book, *Lysis*, to defining *philia*, which he is reluctant to distinguish from erotic love or *erôs*. In *Lysis*, Socrates is in conversation with two youths, Lysis and Menexenus. Socrates tells the youths that, whereas some people desire horses, or dogs, or gold, or honour, he would rather have a good friend than 'the best cock or quail in the world': 'Yea, by the dog of Egypt, I should greatly prefer a real friend to all the gold of Darius, or even to Darius himself: I am such a lover of friends as that.'

Socrates points out that Lysis and Menexenus appear to possess the treasure of friendship in each other, so perhaps Menexenus can tell him: when one person loves another, which of the two becomes the friend of the other, the lover or the beloved? Menexenus replies that either may be the friend of the other, that is, they both are friends. Socrates says that this cannot be the case, since one person may love another who does not love him back, or even who hates him.

Menexenus suggests that, unless they both love each other, neither is a friend. Socrates once again disagrees: if something that does not love in return is not beloved by a lover, then there can be no lovers of things such as horses, dogs, wine, or wisdom. Thus, what is beloved, whether or not it loves in return, may be dear to the lover of it. Such is the case, for example, with children who are too young to love, or who hate their parents for punishing them. This suggests that the beloved is the friend of the lover and the hated is the enemy of the hater, but the implication is then that some people are loved by their enemies and hated by their friends, which seems absurd. Thus, neither the lover nor the beloved can always be said to be a friend to the other.

Socrates suspects that they may have been mistaken in their conclusions, so he turns for guidance to the poets and philosophers, who say that 'like loves like'. He contends that this aphorism must only apply to good people, since bad people are in some way unlike themselves and are just as likely to hate other bad people as everybody else. Thus, good people are friends with other good people, while bad people have no friends. But Socrates remains unconvinced: like cannot be of any use to like, and if people cannot be of any use to one another, they cannot love each other. It remains possible that they love each other because they are both good, but the good is by definition self-sufficient and so has no need or desire for friendship.

What place is there then for friendship if good men, when present, have no use for one another, and, when absent, have no need for one another? How can such persons ever be induced to value one another? Socrates suspects that he may have been wrong in thinking that like loves like. He quotes Hesiod in saying that 'the most like are most full of envy, strife, and hatred of one another, and the most unlike, of friendship'. Menexenus thinks that Hesiod is right in saying that friendship is born out of unlikeness, but Socrates is once again sceptical because the implications are that the enemy is the friend of the friend and the friend the friend of the enemy, and, moreover, that the just man is the friend of the unjust, the good man the friend of the bad, and so on. This, says Socrates, is simply monstrous. Thus, neither like and like, nor unlike and unlike can be friends.

If neither like and like, nor unlike and unlike can be friends, then the friend of the good is neither the good nor the bad, but the neither-good-nor-bad. Since like and like cannot be friends, the neither-good-nor-bad cannot be friends with the neither-good-nor-bad, and since no one can be friends with the bad, the neither-good-nor-bad cannot be friends with the bad either. Thus, the neither-good-nor-bad must be friends with the good, who, says Socrates, are also possessed of beauty, that 'soft, smooth, slippery thing' that 'easily slips in and permeates our souls'. The good and beautiful cannot be friends with the good and beautiful or with the bad, but there is nothing to stop them from being friends with the neither-good-nor-bad. For example, the body is neither good nor bad, but if it is corrupted by sickness, which is bad, then it becomes the friend of the physician. That the body is corrupted by something bad does not make it bad, just as covering Menexenus' auburn locks with white lead does not make them white. Socrates concludes that they have at long last discovered the nature of friendship: 'it is the love which, by reason of the presence of evil, the neither-good-nor-bad has of the good, either in the soul, or in the body, or anywhere.'

However, an unaccountable suspicion comes over him, and he begins to doubt this conclusion. If medicine, which is good, is a friend, then it is a friend for the sake of health. But health is also good, and, if good, then good for the sake of something, something which must also be good, and so on. Surely, there must be some first principle of friendship or dearness for the sake of which all other things are dear. For example, if a father values his son above all things, he also values other things for the sake of his son. If the boy drank poisonous hemlock and the father thought some wine would save him, the father would value the wine and even the vessel that contains the wine. Yet it is not really the wine and the vessel that he would be valuing, but his son. 'That which is only dear to us for the sake of something else is improperly said to be dear, but the truly dear is that in which all these so called dear friendships terminate.' Socrates deduces that the truly dear is the good, but then notices that the good appears to be loved not for its own sake but for the sake of the bad. If the bad were to be eradicated, love and friendship would still flourish, suggesting that there must be some other cause of friendship than the good.

Socrates suggests that this other cause is desire, and that he who desires desires that of which he is in want, and which is therefore dear to him. Thus, desire, love, and friendship appear to be of the congenial, whether in soul, character, manners, or form. And if love is of the congenial, then the true lover must necessarily have his love returned. Unfortunately, this theory falls flat if the congenial is merely the like, since the like cannot be friends with the like.

> So what is to be done? Or rather is there anything to be done? I can only, like the wisemen who argue in courts, sum up the arguments: if neither the beloved, nor the lover, nor the like, nor the unlike, nor the good, nor the congenial, nor any other of whom we spoke—for there were such a number of them that I cannot remember them all—if

none of these are friends, I know not what remains to be said… O Menexenus and Lysis, how ridiculous that you two boys, and I, an old boy, who would fain be one of you, should imagine ourselves to be friends—this is what the bystanders will go away and say—and as yet we have not been able to discover what is a friend!

Lysis may seem to fail in its task of defining friendship, and on one level of course it does. There is, however, far more to *Lysis* than a couple of interesting but misguided thoughts about friendship. By discussing friendship with Lysis and Menexenus as he does, Socrates is not only discussing friendship, but also demonstrating to the youths that, even though they count each other as close friends, they do not really know what friendship is, and that, whatever it is, it is something far deeper and more meaningful than the puerile 'friendship' that they presume to share.

In contrast to the youths, Socrates knows perfectly well what friendship is, and is only feigning ignorance so as to teach the youths: '…and I, an old boy, who would fain be one of you…' More than that, by discussing friendship with Lysis and Menexenus as he does, Socrates is himself in the process of befriending them. He befriends them not with the pleasant banter, gossipy chitchat, or little compliments with which most people befriend one another, but with the kind of philosophical conversation that is the hallmark of the deepest and most meaningful friendships. In the course of this philosophical conversation, he tells the youths that he should 'greatly prefer a real friend to all the gold of Darius', thereby signifying not only that he places friendship on the same high pedestal as philosophy, to which he has devoted (and will sacrifice) his life, but also that the kind of friendship which he has in mind is so rare and uncommon that even he does not possess it.

If friendship ultimately escapes definition, then this is because, like philosophy, friendship is not so much a thing-in-itself as it is a process of becoming. True friends seek together to live truer, fuller lives by relating to each other authentically and by teaching each other about the limitations of their beliefs and the defects in their character, which are a far greater source of error than mere rational confusion. For Socrates as for Plato, friendship and philosophy are aspects of one and the same impulse, one and the same love: the love that seeks to know.

Just as philosophy leads to friendship, so friendship leads to philosophy. In *Phaedrus*, which was most probably written several years after *Lysis*, Socrates and Phaedrus go out into the idyllic countryside just outside Athens and share a long conversation about the anatomy of the soul, the nature of true love, the art of persuasion, and the merits of the spoken over the written word. At the end of this conversation, Socrates offers a prayer to the local deities. This is the famous Socratic Prayer, which is notable both in itself and for the response that it elicits from Phaedrus.

> S: *Beloved Pan, and all ye others gods who haunt this place, give me beauty in the inward soul; and may the outward and inward man be at one. May I reckon the wise to be the wealthy, and may I have such a quantity of gold as a temperate man and he only can bear and carry. —Anything more? The prayer, I think, is enough for me.*

> P: *Ask the same for me, for friends should have all things in common.*

Plato may fail to define friendship in *Lysis*, but in *Phaedrus* he gives us its living embodiment. Socrates and Phaedrus spend their time together enjoying the beautiful Attic countryside while engaging in earnest philosophical conversation. By exercising and building upon reason, they are not only furthering each other's understanding, but also transforming a life of friendship into a life of joint contemplation of those things that are most true and hence most beautiful and most dependable.

At one point, during a lull in their conversation, Socrates insists that they continue talking, lest the cicadas laugh at them for avoiding conversation at midday and mistake them for a pair of slaves who have come to their resting place as cattle to a waterhole. On the other hand, if the cicadas see that their chirruping has not lulled them, they may, out of respect, offer them their god-given gifts. For once upon a time, before the birth of the Muses, the cicadas used to be human beings. Then the Muses were born and song was created, and they were so overwhelmed with the pleasure of singing that they forgot to eat or drink and died without even realizing it. As a gift from the Muses, they were reincarnated as cicadas, singing from the moment they are born to the moment they die without ever feeling hunger or thirst. After dying, the cicadas report back to the Muses in heaven about who is honouring them on earth, and win the love of Terpsichore for the dancers, or Erato for the lovers, and of Calliope, the eldest Muse, for the philosophers.

If only on the basis of his response to the Socratic prayer, it is obvious that Phaedrus is another self to Socrates, since he makes the same choices as Socrates and even justifies making those choices on the grounds that their friendship requires it. Whereas Aristotle tries to tell us what perfect friendship is, Plato lets us feel it in all its allure and transformative power.

24

Love

He whom love touches not walks in darkness.

—Plato

In *Lysis* as elsewhere, Plato is reluctant to distinguish between friendship (*philia*) and erotic love (*erôs*), and he has good reasons for not doing so. Whereas Aristotle is not nearly as interested in erotic love as in friendship, for Plato the best kind of friendship is that which lovers can have for each other. It is a *philia* that is born out of *erôs*, and that in turn feeds back into *erôs* to strengthen and develop it, transforming it from a lust for possession into a shared desire for a higher level of understanding of the self, the other, and the universe. In brief, *philia* transforms *erôs* from a lust for possession into an impulse for philosophy.

As Nietzsche put it,

> *Here and there on earth we may encounter a kind of continuation of love in which this possessive craving of two people for each other gives way to a new desire and lust for possession—a shared higher thirst for an ideal above them. But who knows such love? Who has experienced it? Its right name is friendship.*

In other words, if erotic love can be transformed into the best kind of friendship, it can open up a blissful life of shared understanding in which desire, friendship, and philosophy are in perfect resonance with one another. Plato's theory of love is fleshed out in *Phaedrus* and *Symposium*. Like many Greeks of his era and high social status, Plato is most interested in the same-sex desire that can exist between an older and a younger man, but there is no reason to suppose that his theory of love does not extend to other kinds of erotic relationship. Nonetheless, Plato does distinguish the kind of love that can give rise to *philia* from a baser kind of love that is fallen into (rather than built) by those who are more given to the body than to the soul. Rather than underpin the search for truth, this baser kind of love is almost designed to impede it, and calls into my mind the song of Lenina Crowne in Aldous Huxley's *Brave New World*. In her ditty, Lenina compares love to soma, a hallucinogenic drug engineered to take users on enjoyable, hangover-free 'holidays'. Soma has 'all the advantages of Christianity and alcohol [but] none of their defects'.

> *Hug me till you drug me, honey;*
> *Kiss me till I'm in a coma:*
> *Hug me, honey, snugly bunny;*
> *Love's as good as soma.*

In *Phaedrus*, Socrates says that, although madness can be an illness, it can also be the source of man's greatest blessings. There are four forms of such 'divine madness': prophecy from Apollo, holy prayers and mystic rites from Dionysus, poetry from the Muses, and—the highest form—love from Aphrodite and Eros. The madness of love arises from seeing the beauty of the earth and being reminded of true, universal beauty. Unfortunately, most earthly souls are so corrupted by the body, 'that living tomb which we carry about', that they lose all memory for the universals. When their eyes fall upon the beauty of the earth, they are merely given over to pleasure and 'like a brutish beast' rush on to enjoy and beget. In contrast, the earthly soul that is able to remember true, universal beauty and so to feel true love gazes upon the face of his beloved and reverences it as an expression of the divine: of temperance, justice, and knowledge absolute. As his eyes catch those of his beloved, a shudder passes into an unusual heat and perspiration. The parts of the soul out of which the wings grew, which had hitherto been closed and rigid, begin to melt open, and small wings begin to swell and grow from the root upwards.

> *Like a child whose teeth are just starting to grow in, and its gums are all aching and itching—that is exactly how the soul feels when it begins to grow wings. It swells up and aches and tingles as it grows them.*

The lover feels the utmost joy when he is with his beloved and the most intense longing when they are separated. When they are separated, the parts out of which the lover's wings are growing begin to dry out and close up, and the pain is such that he prizes his beloved above all else. The lover whose soul was once the follower of Zeus among all the other gods seeks out a beloved who shares in his god's philosophical nature, and then does all he can to confirm this nature in him. Thus, the desire of the divinely inspired lover can only be fair and blissful to the beloved. In time, the beloved, who is no common fool, comes to realize that his divinely inspired lover is worth more to him than all his other friends and kinsmen put together, and that neither human discipline nor divine inspiration could have offered him any greater blessing.

> *Thus great are the heavenly blessings which the friendship of a lover will confer upon you ... Whereas the attachment of the non-lover, which is alloyed with a worldly prudence and has worldly and niggardly ways of doling out benefits, will breed in your soul those vulgar qualities which the populace applaud, will send you bowling round the earth during a period of nine thousand years, and leave you a fool in the world below.*

There is in terms of ideas covered much overlap between *Phaedrus* and *Symposium*. In *Symposium*, Socrates argues that, if love is not of nothing, then it is of something, and if it is of something, then it is of something that is desired and therefore of something that is not possessed. Socrates then relates a conversation that he once had with the priestess Diotima of Mantinea, from whom he learnt the art of love. Diotima ('honoured by the gods') told him that the something that love desires but does not possess consists of extremely beautiful and extremely good things, and particularly of wisdom, which is both extremely beautiful and extremely good. Love, said Diotima, must not be confused with the object of love, which, in contrast to love itself, is perfectly beautiful and perfectly good. If love desires but does not possess beautiful and good things, then love cannot, as most people think, be a god. Love is in truth the child of Poverty and Resource, always in need, but always inventive. She is not a god but a great spirit (*daimon*) who intermediates between gods and men. As such, she is neither mortal nor immortal, neither wise nor ignorant, but a lover of wisdom (*philoso-phos*). Just as nobody who is wise wants to become wise, so nobody who is ignorant wants to become wise. 'For herein is the evil of ignorance, that he who is neither good nor wise is nevertheless satisfied with himself: he has no desire for that of which he feels no want.' The aim of loving beautiful and good things is to possess them because the possession of beautiful and good things is happiness, and happiness is an end-in-itself.

Diotima then told Socrates of the proper way to learn to love beauty.* A youth should first be taught to love one beautiful body so that he comes to realize that this beautiful body shares beauty with other beautiful bodies, and thus that it is foolish to love just one beautiful body. In loving all beautiful bodies, the youth comes to understand that the beauty of the soul is superior to the beauty of the body, and begins to love those who are beautiful in soul regardless of whether they are also beautiful in body. Once he has transcended the physical, he gradually finds that beautiful practices and customs and the various kinds of knowledge also share in a common beauty. Finally, he is able to experience beauty itself, rather than the various apparitions of beauty. By exchanging the various apparitions of virtue for virtue itself, he gains immortality and the love of the gods. This is why love is so important, and why it deserves so much praise.

For Aristotle, happiness involves the exercise of reason, because the capacity to reason is the distinctive function of human beings. However, it could be argued that the distinctive function of human beings is in fact the capacity to form nurturing relationships. Plato reconciles these positions by blending desire, friendship, and philosophy into a single total experience that transcends and transforms human existence and connects it with the timeless and universal truths of the eternal and infinite, which is the only form of immortality that is open to man. For Plato, truth and authenticity are a

---

* This is Plato's ladder of love, which I first introduced in Chapter 11 on lust.

higher value than either reason or love, which aim at them, and a higher value even than happiness, which is merely the manifestation of their presence.

25

Kissing

I'll take that winter from your lips.

—Shakespeare

Kissing is not universal among human beings, and, even today, there are some cultures from which it is completely absent. This suggests that it is not innate or intuitive, as it so often seems to us. One possibility is that it is a learned behaviour that evolved from 'kiss feeding', the process by which mothers in some cultures feed their babies by passing masticated food from mouth to mouth. However, there are some contemporary indigenous cultures which practice kiss feeding, but not social or erotic kissing. Another possibility is that it is a culturally determined form of grooming behaviour, or, at least in the case of erotic or deep kissing, a representation, substitute for, and complement to, penetrative intercourse.

Whatever the case, kissing behaviour is not unique to human beings. Primates such as Bonobo apes frequently kiss one another; dogs and cats lick and nuzzle one another as well as members of other species; even snails and insects take part in antennal play. It could be that, rather than kissing, these animals are in fact grooming, smelling, or communicating with one another, but, even so, their behaviour implies and furthers trust and bonding.

Vedic texts from ancient India seem to talk about kissing, and the *Kama Sutra*, which probably dates back to the 2nd century, devotes an entire chapter to modes of kissing. Some anthropologists have suggested that the Greeks learnt about erotic kissing from the Indians when Alexander the Great entered India in 326BC. However, this need not mean that kissing originated in India, nor that it does not predate the oral roots of the Vedic texts. In Homer, which dates back to the 9th century BC, King Priam memorably kisses Achilles' hand to plead for the return of his son's cadaver:

Fear, O Achilles, the wrath of heaven; think on your own father and have compassion upon me, who am the more pitiable, for I have steeled myself as no man yet has ever steeled himself before me, and have raised to my lips the hand of him who slew my son.

In his *Histories*, which date back to the 5th century BC, Herodotus speaks of kissing among the Persians, who greeted men of equal rank with a kiss on the mouth and those of slightly lower rank with a kiss on the cheek. He also reports that, because the Greeks ate of the cow, which was sacred in Egypt, the Egyptians would not kiss them on the mouth.

Kisses also feature in the Old Testament. Disguised as Esau, Jacob kisses the blind Isaac and thereby steals his brother's blessing. In the *Song of Songs*, which seems to celebrate sexual love, one of the lovers implores, "Let him kiss me with the kisses of his mouth, for thy love is better than wine."

Under the Romans, kissing became much more widespread. The Romans kissed their partners or lovers, family and friends, and rulers. They distinguished a kiss on the hand or cheek (*osculum*) from a kiss on the lips (*basium*) and a deep or passionate kiss (*savolium*). Roman poets such as Ovid and Catullus celebrated kissing, as, for example, in Catullus 8:

> *Goodbye girl, now Catullus is firm,*
> *he doesn't search for you, won't ask unwillingly.*
> *But you'll grieve, when nobody asks.*
> *Woe to you, wicked girl, what life's left for you?*
> *Who'll submit to you now? Who'll see your beauty?*
> *Who now will you love? Whose will they say you'll be?*
> *Who will you kiss? Whose lips will you bite?*
> *But you, Catullus, be resolved to be firm.*

Roman kisses fulfilled purposes from the social and political to the sexual. In an age of illiteracy, kisses served to seal agreements, whence the expression 'to seal with a kiss' and the 'X' on the dotted line. The social status of a Roman citizen determined the part of the body on which he could kiss the emperor, from cheek down to foot. Couples got married by kissing in front of a gathered assembly, a practice which has, of course, been carried into modern times.

Practices changed with the decline of Rome and the rise of Christianity. Early Christians often greeted one another with a 'holy kiss', which, they believed, led to a transfer of spirit. The Latin *anima* means both 'breath of air' and 'soul', and, like *animus* ('mind'), derives from the Proto-Indo-European root *ane-* (to breathe, blow). Although St Peter had spoken of the 'kiss of charity' and St Paul of the 'holy kiss', early church sects omitted kissing on Maundy

Thursday, which marks the date on which Judas betrayed Jesus with a kiss: 'But Jesus said unto him, Judas, betrayest thou the Son of man with a kiss?' Outside the Church, kissing was used to consolidate rank and social order, with, for example, subjects and vassals kissing the robe of the king or the ring or slippers of the pope.

After the fall of Rome, the romantic kiss seems to have disappeared for several centuries, only to re-emerge at the end of the 11th century with courtly love. The kiss of Romeo and Juliet is emblematic of this movement, which sought to remove courtship from the purview of family and society, and to celebrate love no longer as a dutiful act but as a liberating and potentially subversive force. Yet, the fate of the star-crossed lovers reminds us that such careless freedom is not without risks, and it could be that vampirism evolved as a representation of the dangers—to health, rank, reputation, prospects, and happiness—of kissing the wrong person.

26

Self-esteem

Nothing is better for self-esteem than survival.

—Martha Gellhorn

'Confidence' comes from the Latin *fidere*, 'to trust'. To be self-confident is to trust in oneself, and, in particular, in one's ability or aptitude to engage successfully or at least adequately with the world. A self-confident person is ready to rise to new challenges, seize opportunities, deal with difficult situations, and take responsibility if and when things go awry. Just as self-confidence leads to successful experience, so successful experience leads to self-confidence. Although any successful experience contributes to our overall confidence, it is, of course, possible to be highly confident in one area, such as cooking or dancing, but very insecure in another, such as mathematics or public speaking.

In the absence of confidence, courage (Chapter 27) takes over. Confidence operates in the realm of the known, courage in that of the unknown, the uncertain, and the fearsome. I cannot be confident in diving from a height of 10 metres unless I once had the courage to dive from a height of 10 metres. Courage is nobler than confidence because it requires greater strength, and because a courageous person is one with limitless capabilities and possibilities. In the lonely hearts columns, single ladies often write that they are looking for a confident man, but what they are really looking for is, of course, a courageous man.

Self-confidence and self-esteem do not always go hand in hand. In particular, it is possible to be highly self-confident and yet to have profoundly low self-esteem, as is the case, for example, with many performers and celebrities. 'Esteem' derives from the Latin *aestimare*, 'to appraise, value, rate, weigh, estimate', and self-esteem is our cognitive and, above all, emotional appraisal of our own worth. More than that, it is the matrix through which we think, feel, and act, and reflects and determines our relation to ourselves, to others, and to the world. In his hierarchy of human needs, psychologist Abraham Maslow featured self-esteem as a deficiency need; and he argued that a person could not meet his growth needs unless he had already met his deficiency needs. To me, it seems that every person is born with a healthy self-esteem, which is then either confirmed or undermined by early and later life experiences.

In the West, self-esteem is primarily based on achievement, whereas in the East (or the traditional East) it is primarily based on 'worthiness', that is, on being seen as an upstanding or dutiful member of the family, community, and other in-groups. In the West, one can get away with being unworthy so long as one is successful; conversely, in the East, one can get away with being unsuccessful so long as one is worthy. One problem with achievement-based self-esteem is that it leads to the fear of failure and the pursuit of 'success' at all costs. Moreover, because achievement is not wholly within our control, it cannot offer a secure foundation for our self-esteem.

Worthiness-based self-esteem also has its drawbacks. First, it relies upon the acceptance of others, and so, like achievement-based self-esteem, is not wholly within our control. Second, because this acceptance is contingent upon conformity, it severely restricts our range of possibilities.

People with a healthy self-esteem do not need to prop themselves up with externals such as income, status, or notoriety, or lean on crutches such as alcohol, drugs, or sex. To the contrary, they treat themselves with respect and take care of their health, community, and environment. They are able to invest themselves completely in projects and people because they do not fear failure or rejection. Of course they suffer hurt and disappointment, but their setbacks neither damage nor diminish them. Owing to their resilience, they are open to growth experiences and meaningful relationships, tolerant of risk, quick to joy and delight, and accepting and forgiving of themselves and others.

It can be instructive to compare healthy self-esteem with pride (Chapter 5), and also with arrogance. If self-confidence is 'I can' and self-esteem is 'I am', then pride is 'I did'. To feel proud is to take pleasure from the goodness of our past actions and achievements. If pride stems from fullness and satisfaction, arrogance stems from hunger and emptiness. 'Arrogance' derives from the Latin *rogare* ('ask, propose'), and means 'to claim for oneself or assume'. Arrogance does not equate to excessive self-esteem, for just as there can be no such thing as excessive health or excessive virtue, so there can be no such thing as excessive self-esteem. To support their self-esteem, arrogant people require constant reassuring and reinforcing both from themselves and others, whence their boastfulness, entitlement, susceptibility, and rigidity or stubbornness. In contrast, people with healthy self-esteem are open and flexible, and in no need of pulling themselves up by pushing others down.

Just as high self-esteem does not amount to arrogance, so poor self-esteem does not amount to humility (Chapter 7). Humble people understand that there is more to life than just themselves, but this need not mean that they suffer from poor self-esteem. While some people with poor or fragile self-esteem are arrogant, most simply suffer in silence. These latter people tend to see the world as a hostile place and themselves as its helpless victims. As a result, they are reluctant to express and assert themselves and miss out on experiences and opportunities, which, in the long run, further undermines their self-esteem. Poor self-esteem can be deeply rooted, sometimes with origins in traumatic childhood experiences such as prolonged separation from parent figures, neglect, or emotional, physical, or sexual abuse. In later life, self-esteem can be undermined by ill health, negative life events such as redundancy or divorce, and long-term psychological and social stressors such as strained relationships and discrimination. The relationship between poor self-esteem and mental disorder is very complex. Poor self-esteem predisposes to mental disorder, which in turn undermines self-esteem. Moreover, poor self-esteem is in itself a symptom of mental disorder, particularly clinical depression and borderline personality disorder.

The Buddhist take on poor self-esteem is that it is akin to a negative emotion or delusion because it leaves us in frantic pursuit of everything except what is truly important, namely, our growth and that of others. Moreover, our agitation is worse than useless since it changes neither the past nor the future but merely makes the present more miserable. The Buddhist notion of diligence is to delight in doing good deeds, and to refrain from such service is a mark of *kausidya* or 'spiritual sloth'. *Kausidya* has three aspects: not doing something out of indolence, not doing something out of faintheartedness, and seeming busy but in reality wasting time and energy on meaningless activities that will not accomplish anything in the long run. It is only by surmounting these three aspects that we can be said to be truly diligent. Tagore, the first non-European to win the Nobel Prize in Literature, seems to capture the Buddhist attitude in this poem-prayer:

Let me not pray to be sheltered from dangers but to be fearless in facing them.
Let me not beg for the stilling of my pain but for the heart to conquer it.
Let me not crave in anxious fear to be saved but hope for the patience to win my freedom.
Grant me that I may not be a coward, feeling your mercy in my success alone; but let me find the grasp of your hand in my failure.

Aside from praying, how might we build our self-esteem? People usually find it easier to build their self-confidence than their self-esteem, and, confusing the one with the other, end up with a long list of abilities and achievements to put to their names. Rather than facing up to their imperfections and failures, they hide them behind their certificates and prizes. But as anyone who has been to university knows, a long list of abilities and achievements is neither sufficient nor necessary for healthy self-esteem. While people keep on working at their list in the hope that it might one day be long enough, they try to fill the emptiness inside them with status, income, possessions, relationships, sex, and so on. Attack their status, criticize their house or car, and observe in their reaction that it is them that you attack and criticize. By the same token, children cannot be built up with empty and condescending praise, inflated grades, and tin trophies. At best, they will feel confused and exasperated; at worst, they will be deterred from the sort of endeavour from which real self-esteem can grow.

And what sort of endeavour is that? Whenever we live up to our hopes and dreams, we can feel ourselves growing. Whenever we fail but know that we have given our all, we can feel ourselves growing. Whenever we stand up for our values and suffer the consequences, we can feel ourselves growing. Whenever we come to terms with a painful truth, we can feel ourselves growing. Whenever we bravely live up to our ideals, we can feel ourselves growing. This is where self-esteem comes from. It comes from bravely living up to our ideals—not from the approval of our parents, or the successes of our children, or the size of our paycheck, or anything else that is not truly our own but, instead, a betrayal of ourselves.

Socrates is a shining example of a man who bravely lived up to his ideals, and, in the end, bravely died for them. Throughout his life, he never lost faith in the mind's ability to discern and decide, and so to apprehend and master reality. Nor did he ever betray truth and integrity for a pitiable life of self-deception and semi-consciousness. In seeking relentlessly to align mind with matter and thought with fact, he remained faithful both to himself and to the world, with the result that he is still alive in this sentence and millions of others that have been written about him. More than a great philosopher, Socrates was the living embodiment of the dream that philosophy might one day set us free.

27

Courage

Where is your ancient courage?

—Shakespeare

There is little point in being anything unless we can also be that thing when it matters most. Courage is the noblest of the virtues because it is the one that guarantees all the others, and the one that is most often mortally missing.

But what is courage? It seems like an easy question, until, that is, we try to answer it. In Plato's *Laches*, Socrates famously sticks the question to the eminent Athenian general Laches. Also present is the Athenian general Nicias. Here is a brief outline of the conversation that ensues:

S: What is courage?
L: Courage is when a soldier is willing to remain at his post and defend himself against the enemy.
S: But a man who flees from his post can also sometimes be called courageous. Aeneas* was always fleeing on horses, yet Homer praised

---

*   A mythological hero of the Trojan War, son of Prince Anchises of Troy and the goddess Aphrodite, and ancestor of Romulus and Remus.

him for his knowledge of fear and called him the 'counsellor of fear'.

L: Perhaps, but these are cases concerning horsemen and chariots, not foot soldiers.

S: Well what about the Spartan hoplites at the Battle of Plataea, who fled the enemy only to turn back once their lines had been broken? In any case, what I really want to know from you is this: what is courage in every instance, for the foot soldier, for the horseman, and for every other class of warrior, not to forget those who are courageous in illness or poverty and those who are brave in the face of pain or fear.

L: How do you mean?

S: Well, what is it that all these instances of courage have in common? For example, quickness can be found in running, in speaking, and in playing the lyre. In each of these instances, 'quickness' can be defined as 'the quality which accomplishes much in little time'. Is there a similar, single definition of courage that can apply to every one of its instances?

L: I suggest that courage is a sort of endurance of the soul.

S: That can't be right. Endurance can be born out of wisdom, but it can also be born out of folly, in which case it is likely to be blameworthy. Courage, by contrast, is always fine and praiseworthy.

L: Very well then, courage is 'wise endurance of the soul'.

S: Who do you think is more courageous, the man who is willing to hold out in battle in the knowledge that he is in a stronger position, or the one in the opposite camp who is willing to hold out nonetheless?

L: The second man, of course—though you are right, his endurance is, of course, the more foolish.

S: Yet foolish endurance is disgraceful and harmful, whereas courage is always a fine and noble thing.

L: I'm thoroughly confused.

S: So am I, Laches. Still, we should persevere in our enquiry so that courage itself won't make fun of us for not searching for it courageously!

L: I'm sure I know what courage is. Of course I do! So why do I seem unable to put it into words?

N: I once heard Socrates say that every person is good with respect to that in which he is wise, and bad in respect to that in which he is ignorant. So perhaps courage is some sort of knowledge or wisdom.

S: Thank you, Nicias. Let's go with that. If courage is some sort of knowledge, of what is it the knowledge?

N: It is the knowledge of the fearful and the hopeful in war, as well as in every other sphere or situation.

L: Nonsense! Wisdom is other than courage. When it comes to illness, it is the physician who knows best what is to be feared but the patient who shows courage. So wisdom and courage can't be the same thing.

N: That's wrong. The physician's knowledge amounts to no more than an ability to describe health and disease, whereas it is the patient who truly knows whether his illness is more to be feared than his recovery. And so it is the patient, and not the physician, who knows best what is to be feared and what is to be hoped.

S: Nicias, if, as you say, courage is the knowledge of the grounds of fear and hope, then courage is very rare among men, while animals can never be called courageous but at most fearless.

N: The same is also true of children. A child who fears nothing because he has no sense can hardly be called courageous.

S: Right, so let's investigate the grounds of fear and hope. Fear is produced by anticipated evil things, but not by evil things that have happened or that are happening. Hope, in contrast, is produced by anticipated good things or by anticipated non-evil things.

N: Right.

S: For any science of knowledge, there is not one science of the past, one of the present, and one of the future. Knowledge of past, present, and future are the same type of knowledge.

N: Of course.

S: Thus, courage is not merely the knowledge of fearful and hopeful things, but the knowledge of all things, including those that are in the present and in the past. A person who had such knowledge could not be said to be lacking in courage, but neither could he be said to be lacking in justice, temperance, or indeed any of the virtues. So, in trying to define courage, which is a part of virtue, we have succeeded in defining virtue itself. Virtue is wisdom—or so it seemed to me just a moment ago.

Courage, says Socrates, is knowledge. Imagine that I am walking along a beach and spot someone drowning. I know that I cannot swim and that there are strong currents in this particular area, but I jump in anyway because a human life is at stake. Very soon, I too need rescuing, and, despite my best intentions, have only succeeded in making a bad situation worse. As I completely misjudged the situation, I acted not bravely but recklessly. The lifeguard, in contrast, is a strong swimmer and equipped with a floater. From past experience, she knows that if she dives in she stands an excellent chance of making a rescue. Of course there is some risk involved, but the potential benefit is so large and likely that it far outweighs the risk. If the lifeguard perfectly understands all this, she will 'courageously' dive in. If she does not dive in, she cannot be said to have a full grasp of the situation.

One of Socrates' most famous arguments is that no one ever knowingly does evil. If people do wrong, it is, ultimately, because they are unable to measure and compare pleasures and pains—not, as many people think, because their ethics are overwhelmed by a desire for pleasure. People do evil because they are ignorant. They act with recklessness or cowardice because such is the limit of their understanding. In the long term, courage maximizes pleasure and minimizes pain, both for ourselves and for those around us, which is why Socrates called it 'a kind of salvation'.

Now, geometry, medicine, and any other field of knowledge can readily be taught and passed on from one person to another. However, this does not seem to be the case with courage and the other parts of virtue, which suggests that Socrates' conclusion in the *Laches* is wrong and that they are not knowledge after all. In the *Meno*, which Plato almost certainly wrote several years after the *Laches*, Socrates argues that people of wisdom and virtue such as Themistocles are in fact very poor at imparting these qualities. Themistocles was able to teach his son Cleophantus skills such as standing upright on horseback and shooting javelins, but no one ever praised Cleophantus for his wisdom and virtue, and the same can be said for Lysimachus and his son Aristides, Pericles and his sons Paralus and Xanthippus, and Thucydides and his sons Melesias and Stephanus. As there do not appear to be any teachers of virtue, it seems that virtue cannot be taught; and if virtue cannot be taught, then it is not, after all, a type of knowledge.

If virtue cannot be taught, how, asks Meno, did good men come about? Socrates replies that he and Meno have so far overlooked that right action is possible under guidance other than that of knowledge. A man who has knowledge of the road to Larisa may make a good guide, but a man who has only correct opinion of the road but has never been and does not know may make just as good a guide.

If he who thinks the truth can be just as good a guide to Larisa as he who knows the truth, then correct opinion can be just as good a guide to right action as knowledge. In that case, how, asks Meno, is knowledge any different from correct opinion? Socrates replies that correct opinions are like the statues of Daedalus*, which had to be tied down so that they would not run away. Correct opinions can be tied down with 'an account of the reason why', whereupon they cease to be correct opinions and become knowledge.

Since virtue is not knowledge, all that remains is for it to be correct opinion. This much explains why virtuous men such as Themistocles, Lysimachus, and Pericles were unable to impart their virtue to their sons. Virtuous people are no different from soothsayers, prophets, and poets, who say many true things when they are inspired but have no real knowledge of what they are saying. If ever there were a virtuous person who was able to impart his virtue to another, he would be said to be among the living as Homer says Tiresias was among the dead: 'he alone has understanding; but the rest are flitting shades.'

Like all virtue, courage consists not in knowledge but in correct opinion. Virtue relates to behaviour, and in particular to good behaviour or ethics. In ethics, the choice of one action over others involves a complex and indeterminate calculus that cannot be condensed into, and hence expressed as, knowledge. Whereas knowledge is precise and explicit, correct opinion is vague and unarticulated and more akin to intuition or instinct. Thus, correct opinion, and so courage, cannot be taught but only ever encouraged or inspired.

---

*   A mythological craftsman of unsurpassed skill and father of Icarus.

From this I conclude that the best education consists not in being taught but in being inspired—which is, I think, a far more difficult thing to do. Unfortunately, it seems that many people are simply not open to being inspired, not even by the most charismatic people or greatest works of art and thought.

As Hemingway scathed, 'He was just a coward and that was the worst luck any man could have.'

28

Ecstasy

Men die in despair, while spirits die in ecstasy.

—Balzac

Happiness is deemed so important as to feature as an unalienable human right in the US Declaration of Independence. It is, however, a fuzzy concept that means different things to different people. On one level, it can be amalgamated with a range of positive or pleasant emotions such as acceptance, contentment, gratitude, excitement, amusement, and joy. On another level, it can be thought of in terms of human flourishing or the good life. I have discussed happiness at some length in *The Art of Failure*, and do not propose to revisit the topic here. Instead, I will concentrate on euphoria and, in particular, on ecstasy.

Euphoria derives from the Greek *eu-* ('good') and *pherein* ('to bear'), and literally means 'to bear well'. The term has come to refer to any form of intense elation or positive feeling, especially that with an abstract or expansive quality. Such intense elation is uncommon in the normal course of human life, but can be induced by certain substances and certain experiences such as beauty, art, music, love, orgasm, exercise, and triumph. It can also stem from a number of psychiatric and neurological disorders, first among them bipolar affective disorder (manic-depressive illness).

The pinnacle of euphoria is ecstasy, which literally means 'to be or stand outside oneself'. Ecstasy is a trance-like state in which consciousness of an object is so heightened that the subject dissolves or merges into the object. Einstein called it the 'mystic emotion', and spoke of it as 'the finest emotion of which we are capable', 'the germ of all art and all true science', and 'the core of the true religious sentiment'.

Man is by nature a religious animal, and most if not all cultures have interpreted ecstasy in terms of divine possession or revelation, or union with the divine. Many traditions seek to bring about religious ecstasy or 'enlightenment' by one of several methods including meditation, intoxication, and ritual dancing. Irreligious people can also experience ecstasy, most often 'by accident'. In this manner, atheists and agnostics are able to experience the deepest religion without getting caught in the trivia and trappings of any one particular religion.

Ecstasy is difficult to describe, in part because it is uncommon. Unless it is induced, it is most likely to supervene in a period of inactivity, particularly a non-routine period of inactivity, or in a novel, unfamiliar, or unusual setting or set of circumstances. The experience is typically described as delightful beyond expression and the first episode as life changing. During an episode, the person enters into a trans-like state that typically lasts from minutes to hours. In that interval, he feels a great sense of calm and quiescence, and may become tearful and unresponsive up to the point of unconsciousness.

One of my friends described the experience thus: "It felt like the fulfillment of my life, but, more than that, the fulfillment of all life, of life itself. It put everything into perspective and gave it all unity, purpose, and nobility... It's completely changed me. Still today, everything I do—and, more importantly, don't do—is grounded in that vision, grounded in that reality... It's as if a channel of light and life has opened up in my mind. I feel more alert and alive, and often experience aftershocks of the original experience. These aftershocks can be set off by the smallest things: the song of a bird, the sun playing into a room, the fleeting expression on the face of a friend, or anything that suddenly reminds me that, yes, I am alive!"

Ecstasy can lead to one or more epiphanies. An epiphany, or 'eureka moment', can be defined as a sudden and striking realization, especially one that is both original and profound. For instance, my friend told me that he had torn up his CV (resumé) after realizing that whatever he could get with a CV was not worth having. In Sanskrit, 'epiphany' is rendered as *bodhodaya*, which derives from *bodha* ('wisdom') and *udaya* ('rising'), and so literally means 'a rising of wisdom'.

The defining feature of ecstasy is perhaps the dissolution of boundaries, with the ego merging into all of being. More than at any other time in human history, our culture emphasizes the sovereign supremacy of the ego and so the ultimate separateness and responsibility of each and every one of us. From a young age, we are taught to remain in tight control of our ego with the aim of projecting it as far out as possible. As a result, we have lost the art of letting go, and, indeed, no longer even recognize the possibility, leading to a poverty or monotony of conscious experience.

True, letting go of the ego can threaten the life that we have built and even the person that we have become, but it can also free us from our modern narrowness and neediness and deliver us into a world that is not only wider but also brighter and richer.

Little children have a quiescent or merged ego, which is why they brim with joy and wonder. Youth and ecstasy are the echoes of a primordial wisdom.

Wonder

When we affirm that philosophy begins with wonder, we are affirming in effect that sentiment is prior to reason.

—Richard Weaver

In Plato's *Theaetetus*, Socrates presents the young Theaetetus with a number of difficult contradictions. This is the exchange that ensues.

S: I believe that you follow me, Theaetetus; for I suspect that you have thought of these questions before now.
T: Yes, Socrates, and I am amazed when I think of them; by the Gods I am! And I want to know what on earth they mean; and there are times when my head quite swims with the contemplation of them.
S: I see, my dear Theaetetus, that Theodorus had a true insight into your nature when he said that you were a philosopher, for wonder is the feeling of a philosopher, and philosophy begins in wonder. He was not a bad genealogist who said that Iris* is the child of Thaumas†...

---

*   The messenger of heaven.
†   Wonder.

In the *Metaphysics*, Aristotle says that it is wonder that led the first philosophers to philosophy, since a man who is puzzled thinks of himself as ignorant and philosophizes to escape from his ignorance. In his commentary on the *Metaphysics*, Aquinas seems to agree, adding that, 'Because philosophy arises from awe, a philosopher is bound in his way to be a lover of myths and poetic fables. Poets and philosophers are alike in being big with wonder.' If Plato, Aristotle, and Aquinas are correct in attributing philosophy—and, by extension, science, religion, art, and all else that transcends everyday existence—to wonder, then it becomes important to ask, what exactly is wonder?

Wonder is a complex emotion involving elements of surprise, curiosity, contemplation, and joy. It is perhaps best defined as a heightened state of consciousness and emotion brought about by something singularly beautiful, rare, or unexpected—that is, by a marvel. 'Marvel' derives from the Latin *mirabilia* ('wonderful things'), and ultimately from the Latin *mirus* ('wonderful'). 'Admire' shares the same root as 'marvel' and originally meant 'to wonder at', although this sense has been steadily attenuated since the 16th century—along, one might say, with wonder itself. Aquinas speaks of philosophers and poets as one because, like philosophers, poets are moved by marvels, with the purpose of poetry being, broadly, to record and in some sense recreate marvels.

Wonder is most similar to awe. However, awe is more explicitly directed at something that is much greater or more powerful than we are. Compared to wonder, awe is more closely associated with fear, respect, reverence, or veneration than with joy. Without this element of respect, reverence, or veneration, all that remains is fear, that is, no longer awe but terror or horror. Awe is also less detached than wonder, which allows for greater and freer contemplation of the object. Other near-synonyms of wonder include astonishment, amazement, and astoundment. In essence, to astonish means to fill with sudden and overpowering surprise or wonder, to amaze means to astonish greatly, and to astound means to amaze greatly. This overbidding ends with dumbfounding, which means—you guessed it—to astound greatly.

Wonder involves significant elements of surprise and curiosity, both of which are forms of interest. Surprise is a spontaneous and short-lived reaction to something unexpected, immediately followed by at least some degree of confusion and one or more emotions such as joy, fear, disappointment, or anger. Surprise spans the divide between expectation and reality, directing our attention to some-thing unforeseen and prompting us to re-examine and revise our concepts and beliefs. 'Surprise' literally means 'overtaken' (Old French *sur* + *prendre*). In the *Tusculan Disputations*, Cicero argues that true sapience is to prepare oneself for every eventuality so as never to be surprised, or overtaken, by anything. Cicero cites the example of the pre-Socratic philosopher Anaxagoras, who, upon being told of the death of his son, said, 'I knew that I begot a mortal.' Curiosity derives from the Latin *cura*, 'care'. To be curious about something is to desire knowledge of that thing. Knowledge extinguishes curi-osity but not wonder. Like Plato and Aristotle, philosopher AN Whitehead noted that 'philosophy begins in wonder', adding that, 'at the end, when philosophic thought has done its best, the wonder remains.' So while wonder involves significant elements of surprise and curiosity, it is other and greater than either.

Wonder can be excited by grand vistas, natural phenomena, human achievement, and extraordinary facts, among others. It is expressed by a bright-eyed stare that is sometimes accompanied by an opening of the mouth and a suspension of the breath. By drawing us out of ourselves, wonder reconnects us with something much greater and higher than our daily humdrum. It is the ultimate homecoming (cf. nostalgia), returning us to the world that we came from and were in danger of losing.

However, notice that this kind of wonder is not quite the same as the more engaged, pregnant kind of wonder that moved Theaetetus to philosophy. This latter kind of wonder, or Socratic wonder, is not so much wonder in the sense of awe as wonder in the sense of puzzlement and perplexity. Rather than grand vistas and such like, it arises from contradictions in thought and language, and goads us on to examine these contradictions in the hope of resolving or at least understanding them.

> *T: Yes, Socrates, and I am amazed when I think of [these questions];*
> *by the Gods I am! and I want to know what on earth they mean; and*
> *there are times when my head quite swims with the contemplation*
> *of them.*

As mentioned in Chapter 7, Socrates himself first turned to philosophy after being bewildered by the Delphic Oracle, which, despite his claims to ignorance, pronounced him the wisest of all men. To discover the meaning of this contradiction, he questioned a number of supposedly wise men and in each case concluded, 'I am likely to be wiser than he to this small extent, that I do not think I know what I do not know.' Wonder in the sense approaching awe is a universal experience found also in children (think of a child at the circus) and perhaps even in higher-order primates and other animals. In contrast, Socratic wonder is much more rarefied, and, as Socrates implies by calling it 'the feeling of a philosopher', not given to everyone. Yet, both kinds of wonder have in common that they are directed at something that is in some sense greater and higher than us, and beyond our grasp.

In his *Advancement of Learning*, Francis Bacon called wonder 'broken knowledge', and there is certainly a sense in which wonder, which may be cognate to the German *Wunde* ('wound'), breaches or exposes us. This breach requires filling or repairing, not only by philosophy but also by science, religion, and art, giving rise to a third and even more exalted kind of wonder, which is the wonder of discovery and creation. Culture does not sate but nourishes wonder. Scientific theories and discoveries such as the Big Bang theory and the periodic table of the elements are often more wondrous than the perplexities that they intended to solve. Religious buildings and rituals make us feel small and insignificant while at the same time elevating and inspiring us. Wonder begets culture, which begets yet more wonder, and the end of wonder is wisdom, which is the state of perpetual wonder.

Sadly, many people do not open themselves to wonder for fear that it may distract them, overwhelm their resources, or upset their equilibrium. After all, wonder is wounding, and *thauma* is only one letter off 'trauma'. To wonder is also to wander, to stray from society and its norms and constructs, to be alone, to be free—which is, of course, deeply subversive and why even organized religions need to tread a fine line with wonder. To rationalize the fear of it, wonder is dismissed as a childish and self-indulgent emotion that is to be grown out of rather than encouraged or cultivated.

So much is true, that children brim with wonder, before it is leached out of them by need and neurosis. Today, most young people who go to university do so for the sake not of learning or marveling but of improving their career prospects, and so pass by the wonder and wisdom that might have saved them from needing a career in the first place. According to Matthew, Jesus said, 'Suffer little children, and forbid them not, to come unto me: for of such is the kingdom of heaven.'

> *Verily I say unto you, except ye be converted, and become as little children, ye shall not enter into the kingdom of heaven ... whoso shall offend one of these little ones which believe in me, it were better for him that a millstone were hanged about his neck, and that he were drowned in the depth of the sea.*

Notes

Epigraph
1.   John Milton, *Paradise Lost*, Bk 1: 254–255.

Introduction
2.   Quoted in Marcel Haedrich (1972): *Coco Chanel: Her Life, Her Secrets*, Ch 1. Trans. Charles Lam Markmann. Little Brown and Co.
3.   Aristotle, *Rhetoric*, Bk 2 Ch 1–11.
4.   *Book of Rites (Liji)*, Ch 9.
5.   Ekman P, Friesen WV, & Ellsworth P (1982): *What emotion categories or dimensions can observers judge from facial behaviour?* In P Ekman (Ed.), *Emotion in the Human Face*, pp. 39–55. Cambridge University Press.
6.   Plutchik R, *The Emotions* (Revised edition, 1991). University Press of America.
7.   G Flaubert (1950), *Madame Bovary*, p120. Trans. A. Russell. Harmondsworth: Penguin.
8.   W James (1884): *What is an emotion?* Mind 9, 188–205.
9.   *Ibid.*
10. Schachter S & Singer J (1962): *Cognitive, social, and physiological determinants of emotional state*. Psychological Review 69: 379–399.

11. D Hume (1738): *A Treatise of Human Nature* II.3.3, 415.

12. Aristotle, *Nicomachean Ethics*, Bk 10. Trans. WD Ross.

1: Boredom

13. F de La Rochefoucauld (1665–1678), *Reflections; or Sentences and Moral Maxims*, Maxim 304.

14. E Fromm, *The Theory of Aggression*, p. 7. Written by Fromm to introduce his book *The Anatomy of Human Destructiveness*, first published in the New York Times Magazine in February 1972.

15. As quoted in P Toohey (2012), *Boredom: A Lively History*. Yale University Press.

16. Aquinas, *Summa Theologica* II–II, 35, 3.

17. C Wilson (1984), *A Criminal History of Mankind*, p. 610. Panther Books.

18. A Schopenhauer, *On the Vanity of Existence* (from *Essays*).

19. PwC (2012), *Global entertainment and media outlook: 2012–2016*.

20. B Russell (1930), *The Conquest of Happiness*, Ch 4 Boredom and excitement.

21. S Sontag (1977), *On Photography*, p42. Farrar, Straus and Giroux.

22. Thich Nhat Hanh (1991), *The Miracle of Mindfulness*. Rider Books.

23. J Boswell (1791), *The Life of Samuel Johnson, LL.D.*

2: Loneliness

24. Byron (1812–1818), *Childe Harold's Pilgrimage*, Canto the Third, XC.

25. McPherson M (2006), *Social isolation in America: Changes in core discussion networks over two decades*. American Sociological Review 71 (3), 353–75.

26. A Chekhov, *Note-Book of Anton Chekhov* (1921). Trans. SS Koteliansky and Leonard Woolf.

27. F Nietzsche (1886), *Beyond Good and Evil*, Ch 2, 49. Trans. Helen Zimmern.

28. F Nietzsche (1881), *The Dawn of Day*, 491. Trans. John McFarland Kennedy.

29. RM Rilke (1902), Letter to Paula Modersohn-Becker dated February 12, 1902. Trans. Jane Bannard Greene and MD Herter Norton.

30. A Storr (1988), *Solitude*, p202. Flamingo.

3: Laziness

31. A Christie (1977), *An Autobiography*.

32. Bible, OT, *Ecclesiastes* 10:18–19 (KJV).

33. Hsee CK et al. (2010), *Idleness aversion and the need for justifiable busyness*. Psychological Science 21(7): 926–930.

34. A Camus (1942), *The Myth of Sisyphus*.

35. O Wilde (1891), *The Critic as Artist: With Some Remarks Upon the Importance of Doing Nothing*.

36. W Shakespeare (c. 1607), *Antony and Cleopatra*, Act III Sc. 11.

4: Embarrassment, Shame, and Guilt

37. A de Noailles (1924), *Poème de l'amour*, CXX.

38. Bible, OT, *Ecclesiastes* 1:2 (VUL).

39. Bible, OT, *Ecclesiastes* 1:2 (KJV).

40. Bible, OT, *Proverbs* 16:18 (KJV).

41. Albertanus of Brescia (1238), *De amore et dilectione Dei et proximi et aliarum rerum et de forma vitae (On love…)*, Bk IV Ch IV *De superbia (On pride)*.

42. Tracy JC & Matsumoto D (2008): *The spontaneous expression of pride and shame: Evidence for biologically innate non-verbal*

displays. Proceedings of the National Academy of Sciences 105: 11655–11660.

43. Aristotle, *Nicomachean Ethics*, Bk IV Ch 3. Trans. WD Ross.

44. *Ibid.*

45. *Ibid.*

46. *Ibid.*

5: *Pride*

47. B Jonson (1602), *Sejanus His Fall*.

48. JP Sartre (1944), *No Exit*.

6: *Humiliation*

49. Bernard of Clairvaux, *Sermons on the Song of Songs*, Sermon 34.

50. Lactantius, *De mortibus persecutorum*, Ch V.

51. I Kant (1797), *Fundamental Principles of the Metaphysics of Morals*.

7: *Humility*

52. Plato, *Apology*. Trans. Benjamin Jowett.

53. R Descartes (1637), *La géometrie* (appendix to the *Discours de la méthode*).

54. Bible, OT, *Isaiah* 14:12–15 (KJV).

55. Bible, OT, *Numbers* 12:13 (KJV).

56. Bible, OT, *Proverbs* 3:34 (KJV).

57. Bible, NT, *Matthew* 23:12 (KJV).

58. Augustine of Hippo, as quoted in *Manipulus Florum* (c. 1306), edited by Thomas of Ireland.

59. Augustine of Hippo, *Sermon 19:2 on the New Testament*.

60. Bhagavad Gita, 18:20–22.

61. D Hume (1751), *An Enquiry Concerning the Principles of Morals*, IX.I.

62. F Nietzsche (1887), *On the Genealogy of Morality*, First Essay.
63. Morris J et al. (2005): *Bringing humility to leadership: Antecedents and consequences of leader humility*. Human Relations 58.10: 1323–1350.

8: Gratitude

64. GK Chesterton (1917), *A Short History of England*, Ch. 6.
65. JB Massieu, *Letter to Abbé Sicard*.
66. G Simmel (1908), *Faithfulness and Gratitude*
67. Seneca, *Moral Letters to Lucilius*, On Worldliness and Retirement. Trans. RM Gummere.
68. Cicero, *Oratio pro Cn. Plancio*, 80.
69. McCullough ME et al. (2002): *The grateful disposition: A conceptual and empirical topography*. Journal of Personality and Social Psychology, 82:112–127.
70. Wood AM et al. (2009): *Gratitude predicts psychological well-being above the Big Five facets*. Personality and Individual Differences, 45:655–660.
71. Wood AM et al (2007): *Coping style as a psychological resource of grateful people*. Journal of Social and Clinical Psychology, 26:1108–1125.
72. Shakespeare, *King Lear*, I–4.
73. D Hume (1738), *A Treatise of Human Nature*, III–I.
74. I Kant (2001), *Lectures on Ethics*. Cambridge University Press.

9: Envy

75. Aeschylus, *Agamemnon*, line 832.
76. J Epstein (2003), *Envy*. Oxford University Press.
77. Dante, *The Divine Comedy*, Purgatory XIII.
78. NW Aldrich Jr. (1988), *Old Money: The Mythology of Wealth in America*. Alfred A. Knopf.

79. Homer, *Iliad*, *24:25–30*.

80. Bible, OT, *Wisdom of Solomon* 2:24 (KJV).

81. Bible, OT, *Genesis* 4:4–8 (KJV).

82. B Russell (1930), *The Conquest of Happiness*.

83. Aristotle, *Rhetoric*, Bk. 2.

84. Bible, OT, *Proverbs* 24:17–18 (KJV).

85. C Bukowski (Nov 1971), Letter to Steven Richmond.

86. Aristotle, *Rhetoric*, Bk. 2.

10: Greed

87. I Illich (1973), *Tools for Conviviality*, Ch. 3.

88. M Friedman (1980), *Free to Choose* television series.

89. Dante, *Divine Comedy*, Purgatory XX.

90. Bible, NT, *Timothy* 6:10.

91. *Mahabharata*, Santi Parva, CLVIII. Trans. Sri Kisari Mohan Ganguli.

11: Lust

92. Marquis de Sade, *Histoire de Juliette, ou les Prospérités du vice*, pt. 2.

93. Bible, NT, *Matthew* 5:27–28 (KJV).

94. Bible, NT, *Corinthians* 7:7 (KJV).

95. Bible, OT, *Ecclesiastes* 7:25–26 (KJV).

96. Dante, *The Divine Comedy*, Inferno V.

97. Shakespeare, Sonnet 129.

98. A Schopenhauer (1818), *The World as Will and Representation*.

99. Bhagavad Gita, 3:36–43.

100. C. Baudelaire, as quoted in J Richardson (1994), *Baudelaire*, p50.

101. I Kant, *The Philosophy of Law*, translated by W. Hastie, in *Morality and Moral Controversies* (1993), 3rd edition, ed by John Arthur. Prentice Hall.

102. K Amis (1963), *One Fat Englishman*. Gollancz.
103. Shakespeare, Sonnet 129.
104. C. Baudelaire, as quoted in J Richardson (1994), *Baudelaire*, p50.
105. Plato, *Symposium*.

12: Sadomasochism
106. JJ Rousseau (1782), *Confessions*.
107. Fedoroff, PJ (2008): *Sadism, sadomasochism, sex, and violence*. Canadian Journal of Psychiatry (Canadian Psychiatric Association) 53(10):637–646.
108. Nordling N et al. (2006): *Differences and similarities between gay and straight individuals involved in the sadomasochistic subculture*. J Homosex. 50(2–3):41–57.
109. Marquis de Sade (1791), *Histoire de Juliette, ou les Prospérités du vice*.
110. L von Sacher-Masoch (1870), *Venus in Furs*.
111. JJ Rousseau (1782), *Confessions*.
112. G Pico della Mirandola (1495), *Disputationes*.
113. JH Meibom (1639), *Treatise on the Use of Flogging in Medicine and Venery*.
114. R von Krafft-Ebing (1886), *Psychopathia Sexualis*.
115. S Freud (1905), *Three Essays on the Theory of Sexuality*.
116. H Havelock Ellis (1897–1928), *Studies in the Psychology of Sex*.
117. G Deleuze (1967), *Coldness and Cruelty*.
118. Bible, OT, *Leviticus* 16.
119. R Byrne (2014), *Aesthetic Sexuality*. Bloomsbury Academic.
120. Terence, *The Self-Tormentor*, Act 1 Sc. 1. *Homo sum: humani nihil a me alienum puto*.

13: Desire

121. W. Somerset Maugham (1920), *Rain*.

122. Bible, OT, *Genesis* 1:3.

123. Rig Veda, Bk 10, hymn 129.

124. D Hume (1738), *A Treatise on Human Nature*.

125. Krishnamurti (1975), *The Beginnings of Learning*, Pt. 2 Ch. 8. Phoenix (2003).

126. Bhagavad Gita, 3:41.

127. A Schopenhauer (1818): *The World As Will And Representation*, Vol. 2, 573. Trans. RB Haldane and J Kemp, 1883.

128. A Schopenhauer (1818), *The World as Will and Representation*, Vol. 2, 557.

129. A Schopenhauer (1818), *The World as Will and Representation*, Vol. 2, 208–10.

130. A Schopenhauer (1839), *On the Freedom of the Will. Der Mensch kann tun was er will; er kann aber nicht wollen was er will.*

131. A Schopenhauer (1851), *The Wisdom of Life*. Trans. T. Bailey Saunders, Echo Library (2006).

132. Diogenes Laertius, *Lives and Opinions of Eminent Philosophers*, Bk 6.

14: Hope

133. Attributed to Aristotle by Diogenes Laertius, *Lives and Opinions of Eminent Philosophers*, Bk 5.

134. Plato, *Protagoras*.

135. Aesop, *The Spendthrift and the Swallow*. Trans. GF Townsend.

136. The principal source for Pandora is Hesiod, *Works and Days*, lines 60–105.

137. Bible, NT, *Corinthians* 13:13 (KJV).

138. Dante, *The Divine Comedy*, Inferno 3.

139. M Luther (1569), *Table Talk*, 298. Trans. W. Hazlitt (1848 edition).

140. A Camus (1942), *The Myth of Sisyphus*. *La lutte elle-même vers les sommets suffit à remplir un coeur d'homme. Il faut s'imaginer Sisyphe heureux.*

15: Nostalgia

141. Bible, OT, *Psalms* 137 (KJV).

142. A Brink (1975), *An Instant in the Wind*.

143. Virgil, *Aeneid*, 1.461 ff.

144. JJ Rousseau (1767), *Dictionnaire de musique*.

145. Zhou X et al. (2012): *Heartwarming memories: Nostalgia maintains physiological comfort*. Emotion 12(4):700.

146. W Whitman, *Song of the Universal*, final verses.

147. CS Lewis, *The Pilgrim's Regress*, afterword to the third edition (1944).

148. CS Lewis (1941), *The Weight of Glory*.

16: Ambition

149. Marcus Aurelius, *Meditations*, 7:3.

150. B Spinoza (1677), *Ethics*, Proposition 29.

151. Plato, *Republic*, Bk. 7.

152. Aristotle, *Nicomachean Ethics*, Bk. 2. Trans. WD Ross.

153. Aristotle, *Nicomachean Ethics*, Bk. 4.

154. Aristotle, *Politics*, Bk. 2.

155. F Bacon (1625), *Essays*, Of Ambition.

156. *Ibid.*

157. Judge, TA & Kammeyer-Mueller, JD (2012): *On the value of aiming high: The causes and consequences of ambition*. Journal of Applied Psychology 97:758–775.

158. Aristotle, *Rhetoric*, Bk. 2. Trans. W. Rhys Roberts.

159. A Christie (1939), *And Then There Were None*.

160. T Mann (1912), *Death in Venice*.

17: Anger

161. D Adams (1980), *The Hitchhiker's Guide to the Galaxy: The Restaurant at the End of the Universe*. Pan Books.

162. RC Solomon (1976), *The Passions*. Doubleday.

163. S Freud (1915), *Instincts and their Vicissitudes*.

164. Plato, *Philebus*.

165. Plato, *Timaeus*.

166. Aristotle, *Nicomachean Ethics*, Bk. 2.

167. Aristotle, *Rhetoric*, Bk. 2.

18: Patience

168. Horace, Carm. 1.24.

169. Bible, OT, *Proverbs* 16:32 (KJV).

170. Bible, OT, *Proverbs* 25:12 (KJV).

171. Bible, OT, *Ecclesiastes* 7:8–9 (KJV).

172. Bible, NT, 1 Thessalonians 5:14–15 (KJV).

173. Krishnan S and Sitaraman R (2012): *Video Stream Quality Impacts Viewer Behavior*. ACM Internet Measurement Conference, Nov 2012.

174. Mischel W et al. (1972): *Cognitive and attentional mechanisms in delay of gratification*. Journal of Personality and Social Psychology 21(2): 204–218.

175. J de la Bruyère (1688), *Les Caractères, Des jugements*, aphorism 108.

176. Kidd C et al. (2013): *Rational snacking: Young children's decision-making on the marshmallow task is moderated by beliefs about environmental reliability*. Cognition 126(1):109–114.

19: Depression

177. Elizabeth II of the United Kingdom (2001). Message from the Queen read by the British ambassador to Washington, Sir Christopher Meyer, on 22 September 2001.
178. M Proust (1927): *In Search of Lost Time: The Past Recaptured*.

20: Fear and anxiety

179. S Kierkegaard (1844), *The Concept of Anxiety*.
180. P Tillich (1952), *The Courage to Be*.
181. Plato, *Phaedo*.

21: Empathy

182. Aristotle, *On the Soul*.
183. J Steinbeck (1941), *The Forgotten Village*, Preface. Viking.
184. Zhuangzi and AC Graham (1981), *The Seven Inner Chapters and other writings from the book of Chuang-tzu*, 123. George Allen and Unwin.

22: Altruism

185. V Woolf (1919), *Night and Day*, Ch. 9.

23: Friendship

186. Aristotle, *Nicomachean Ethics*, Bk 8. Trans. WD Ross.
187. Aristotle, *Nicomachean Ethics*, Bk 8. Trans. RC Bartlett and SD Collins. The University of Chicago Press, 2012.
188. Aristotle, *Nicomachean Ethics*, Bk 8. Trans. WD Ross.
189. Plato, *Lysis*. Trans. Benjamin Jowett.
190. *Ibid.*
191. *Ibid.*
192. *Ibid.*
193. *Ibid.*

194. *Ibid.*

195. Plato, *Phaedrus*. Trans. Benjamin Jowett.

24: Love

196. Plato, *Symposium*. Trans. Benjamin Jowett.

197. F Nietzsche (1882), *The Gay Science*, 1–14.

198. A Huxley (1931), *Brave New World*, Ch. 3.

199. Plato, *Phaedrus*. Trans. Benjamin Jowett.

200. Plato, *Phaedrus*. Trans. Alexander Nehamas and Paul Woodruff.

201. Plato, *Phaedrus*. Trans. Benjamin Jowett.

202. Plato, *Symposium*. Trans. Benjamin Jowett.

25: Kissing

203. Shakespeare (c. 1602), *Troilus and Cressida*, Act IV Sc. 5.

204. Vātsyāyana, *Kama Sutra*, Part 2 Ch. 3, On Kissing.

205. Homer, *Iliad*, Bk. 24. Trans. Samuel Butler.

206. Herodotus, *Histories* 1.134.

207. Herodotus, *An Account of Egypt*.

208. Bible, OT, *Song of Solomon* 1:2 (KJV).

209. Catullus 8, Trans. AS Kline.

210. Bible, NT, *Luke* 22:48.

26: Self-esteem

211. M Gellhorn (1978), *Travels with Myself and Another: A Memoir*. Tarcher (2001).

212. R Tagore (1916), *Fruit-Gathering*, 79.

27: Courage

213. Shakespeare (c. 1606), *Coriolanus*, Act IV Sc. 3

214. Plato, *Laches*.

215. Plato, *Meno*.

216. E Hemingway (1940), *For Whom the Bell Tolls*, Ch. 40.

28: Ecstasy

217. H de Balzac (1835), *Seraphita*, Ch. 3.

218. A Einstein, as quoted in P Barker and CG Shugart (1981), *After Einstein: Proceedings of the Einstein Centennial Celebration*, p179. Memphis State University Press.

29: Wonder

219. R Weaver (1948), *Ideas have Consequences*. University of Chicago Press, 2013.

220. Plato, *Theaetetus*. Trans. Benjamin Jowett.

221. Aristotle, *Metaphysics*, Alpha.

222. Aquinas, *Commentary on Aristotle's Metaphysics*, Bk. 1, Lesson 3, 4.

223. Cicero, *Tusculan Disputations* 3:30.

224. AN Whitehead (1938), *Modes of Thought*, Lecture 8.

225. Plato, *Theaetetus*. Trans. Benjamin Jowett.

226. Plato, *Apology*. Trans. GMA Grube.

227. F Bacon (1605), *The Advancement of Learning*, Ch. 1.

228. Bible, NT, *Matthew* 19:14 (KJV).

229. Bible, NT, *Matthew* 18:3, 18:6 (KJV).

By the same author

Hide and Seek, The Psychology of Self-Deception
ISBN 978-0-9560353-6-3

Self-deception is common and universal, and the cause of most human tragedies. Of course, the science of self-deception can help us to live better and get more out of life. But it can also cast a murky light on human nature and the human condition, for example, on such exclusively human phenomena as anger, depression, fear, pity, pride, dream making, love making, and god making, not to forget age-old philosophical problems such as selfhood, virtue, happiness, and the good life. Nothing could possibly be more important.

The Art of Failure, The Anti Self-Help Guide
ISBN 978-0-9560353-3-2

We spend most of our time and energy chasing success, such that we have little left over for thinking and feeling, being and relating. As a result, we fail in the deepest possible way. We fail as human beings.

The Art of Failure explores what it means to be successful, and how, if at all, true success can be achieved.

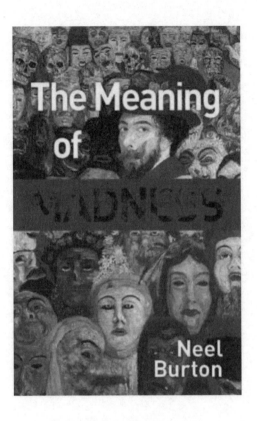

The Meaning of Madness
ISBN 978-0-9560353-0-1

This book proposes to open up the debate on mental disorders, to get people interested and talking, and to get them thinking. For example, what is schizophrenia? Why is it so common? Why does it affect human beings and not animals? What might this tell us about our mind and body, language and creativity, music and religion? What are the boundaries between mental disorder and 'normality'? Is there a relationship between mental disorder and genius? These are some of the difficult but important questions that this book confronts, with the overarching aim of exploring what mental disorders can teach us about human nature and the human condition.

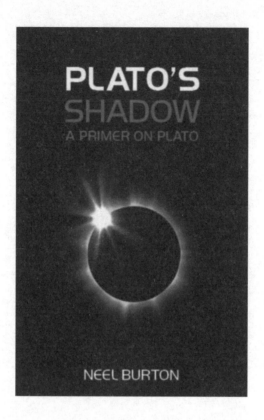

Plato's Shadow – A Primer on Plato
ISBN 978-0-9560353-2-5

Plato thought that only philosophy could bring true understanding, since it alone examines the presuppositions and assumptions that other subjects merely take for granted. He conceived of philosophy as a single discipline defined by a distinctive intellectual method, and capable of carrying human thought far beyond the realms of common sense or everyday experience. The unrivalled scope and incisiveness of his writings as well as their enduring aesthetic and emotional appeal have captured the hearts and minds of generation after generation of readers. Unlike the thinkers who came before him, Plato never spoke with his own voice. Instead, he presented readers with a variety of perspectives to engage with, leaving them free to reach their own, sometimes radically different, conclusions. 'No one,' he said, 'ever teaches well who wants to teach, or governs well who wants to govern.'

This book provides the student and general reader with a comprehensive overview of Plato's thought. It includes an introduction to the life and times of Plato and – for the first time – a précis of each of his dialogues, among which the *Apology, Laches, Gorgias, Symposium, Phaedrus, Phaedo, Meno, Timaeus, Theaetetus, Republic*, and 17 others.

Index